CIVIL PROCEDURE 2010

Special Supplement to the 2010 Edition

Up–to–date generally to April 30, 2010

TO ACCESS THE WHITE BOOK UPDATING SERVICE VIA HTTP://WWW.SWEETANDMAXWELL.CO.UK/WHITEBOOK YOU NEED TO ENTER THE FOLLOWING PASSWORD:
WB2010

SWEET & MAXWELL THOMSON REUTERS

Published in 2010 by Thomson Reuters (Legal) Limited
(Registered in England & Wales, Company No 1679046.
Registered Office and address for service:
100 Avenue Road, London, NW3 3PF) trading as Sweet & Maxwell.
Table of International and European Legislation typeset by Hobbs the Printers Ltd, Totton, Hampshire. All other typesetting by Sweet & Maxwell electronic publishing system.
Printed in the UK by CPI William Clowes, Beccles NR34 7TL.
For further information on our products and services, visit
www.sweetandmaxwell.co.uk.

No natural forests were destroyed to make this product; only farmed timber was used and replanted.

British Library Cataloguing in Publication Data
A catalogue record for this book is available from the British Library

ISBN-978-0-41404-267-4

JOAN GOULBOURN
Of the Public Guardianship Office

R. JAY
Solicitor

E. JEARY
Of the Court Funds Office

MASTER JERVIS KAY
Admiralty Registrar and a Master of the Senior Courts, Queen's Bench Division; One of Her Majesty's Counsel

DISTRICT JUDGE M. LANGLEY
A District Judge of the Central London County Court

C. LEWIS Q.C.
Barrister

HIS HONOUR JUDGE MACKIE C.B.E., Q.C.
London Mercantile Court

KARON MONAGHAN Q.C.
Barrister, Matrix Chambers

HELEN MOUNTFIELD
Barrister, Matrix Chambers

MASTER J. O'HARE
A Master of the Senior Courts Costs Office

HER HONOUR JUDGE PATRICIA PEARL
A Circuit Judge on the South Eastern Circuit

MASTER ROBERTS
A Master of the Senior Courts, Queen's Bench Division

DISTRICT JUDGE RICHARD ROBINSON
Principal Registry of the Family Division

MASTER ROSE
A Master of the Senior Courts, Queen's Bench Division (retired)

C. SANDERS
Of the Official Solicitor and Public Trustee

IAN SEWELL
Costs Clerk, Supreme Court of the United Kingdom

K. TALBOT
Barrister, Member of the New York Bar

MASTER TEVERSON
A Master of the Senior Courts, Chancery Division

MASTER VENNE
Registrar of Criminal Appeals and Master of the Crown Office

RICHARD WALFORD
Barrister, Serle Court Chambers

TIM WALLIS
Mediator and Solicitor with Expedite Resolution and Trust Mediation

H. WARD
Barrister

GARY WEBBER
Barrister and Mediator and a Deputy District Judge

GORDON WIGNALL
Barrister

DR VICTORIA WILLIAMS
A Deputy Master of the Senior Courts Costs Office; Barrister, Coram Chambers

CHIEF MASTER WINEGARTEN
Chief Master of the Senior Courts, Chancery Division

MASTER YOXALL
A Master of the Senior Courts, Queen's Bench Division

ADVISORY EDITORS

PREFACE

On April 20, 2007 the Department of Constitutional Affairs issued a Consultation Paper entitled "Case track limits and the claims process for personal injury claims" (CP8/07) in which the second of the matters raised was the efficiency of the existing rules of practice and procedure for dealing with personal injury cases where liability is admitted by defendants supported by insurers, and the main issues requiring determination by the court if not settled by agreement between the parties relate to the amount of damages to be awarded. The Consultation Paper considered how the procedures for handling these cases could be streamlined to make the overall process (from pre–action protocol requirements to trial procedures) not only more efficient but also cost–effective, and set out proposals "for a new system based around the principles of early notification of a claim, the promotion of early admissions of liability and the removal of duplication of work from the process". The proposals also aimed to deal with the problem of "frontloading of costs" in such cases.

The product of this second part of the Consultation Paper is the introduction of an innovative new scheme setting out the pre–action conduct expected of parties to personal injury claims, and in particular of their legal representatives and insurers. The heart of the new scheme is the Pre–Action Protocol for Low Value Personal Injury Claims in Road Traffic Accidents ("the RTA Protocol") and a new CPR Pt 8 alternative procedure (bordering on the summary) for determining disputes as to quantum, and specially designed to complement the Protocol processes where defendants' insurers and claimant parties and their legal representatives have been unable to reach agreement ("the Stage 3 Procedure"). The Protocol applies to cases in which the claimant claims damages valued at no more than £10,000 as a result of a personal injury sustained in a road traffic accident occurring on or after April 30, 2010. The new Pt 8 procedure is set out in a new practice direction supplementing that Part. The Protocol and the practice direction are to be published in TSO CPR Update 52. The scheme incorporates a fixed costs regime, special arrangements for the making of offers to settle (including pre–action offers), and the costs consequences thereof, and for the withdrawal of pre–action admissions. The necessary amendments to the CPR to effect these aspects of the scheme are made by the Civil Procedure (Amendment) Rules 2010. The principal amendments are the addition to Pt 36 (Offers to Settle) of Section II (RTA Protocol Offers to Settle), and the addition to Pt 45 (Fixed Costs) of Section VI (Pre–Action Protocol for Low Value Personal Injury Claims in Road Traffic Accidents). As is noted in the commentary in para.C13A–005 herein, the structure of this new material reverses the structure that normally obtains in that, in effect, a pre–action protocol is supplemented by a practice direction, which in turn, and together with the protocol, are supplemented by CPR rules.

The content of the RTA Protocol, the Practice Direction and the statutory instrument amending the CPR (all of which come into effect on April 30, 2010), were not finalised by the relevant authorities until the end of February 2010, too late to be included in their appropriate places in the 2010 edition of the *White Book* (published on March 31, 2010). For obvious reasons, the Editors were keen that the new material, with expert commentary, should be made available to subscribers before the commencement date and are pleased that the publishers have been able to accomplish that by publishing this special supplement.

In producing the supplement for the purposes explained above the opportunity has been taken to include some other material coming to hand after the 2010 edition had gone to press; in particular, amendments recently made to the Court Funds Rules 1987 (see also *CP News* Issue 03/2010 March 8, 2010).

The changes to rules, practice directions and pre–action protocols referred to in this supplement come into effect on April 30, 2010, with the exceptions of the amendments to the Court Funds Rules 1987 (see para.6A–93), to Section III of Pt 65 (see para.65PD.5) and to the Pre–Action Protocol for Possession Claims Based on Rent Arrears (see para.C11–001) which came into effect on April 1, 2010.

Professor I.R Scott
General Editor
March 2010

SERVICE INFORMATION

Generally up-to-date to April 30, 2010

This is a Special Supplement offered as part of your *White Book* subscription. It is important that subscribers should understand that this publication is additional to, and does not take the place of, the forthcoming First Supplement. Content in this Special Supplement will be included in the First Cumulative Supplement which will publish as normal in June 2010.

This Special Supplement is published for the purpose of taking account principally of a new Pre–Action Protocol for Low Value Personal Injury Claims in Road Traffic Accidents and an associated new CPR Part 8 Practice Direction, plus amendments made to the Civil Procedure Rules introduced by the Civil Procedure (Amendment) Rules 2010 and TSO CPR Update 52.

The new provisions come into force generally on April 30, 2010 and include, with commentary:

- A new Practice Direction on Low Value Personal Injury Claims in Road Traffic Accidents to Part 8 (Alternative Procedure for Claims);
- A new Pre–Action Protocol for Low Value Personal Injury Claims in Road Traffic Accidents;
- New sections added to Part 36 (Offers to Settle) and Part 45 (Fixed Costs); and
- Amendments made to Part 14 (Admissions), Part 21 (Children and Protected Parties), Part 27 (Small Claims) and the Pre–Action Protocol for Personal Injury Claims.

Amendments have also been made in respect of social housing, which include changes to:

- Part 55 (Possession Claims);
- Part 65 (Anti–Social Behaviour and Harassment); and
- Pre–Action Protocols for Possession Claims Based on Rent Arrears and Mortgage or Home Purchase Plan Arrears in respect of Residential Property.

Separately, amendments are made to the Court Funds Rules introduced by the Court Funds (Amendment) Rules 2010 (SI 2010/172).

To access the *White Book Updating Service*, please visit **http://www.sweetandmaxwell.co.uk/whitebook**. Click on "Login to the White Book Updating Service", enter your password (printed in the preliminary pages in both Volumes of *Civil Procedure*) and click on What's New.

Forms

The Forms Volume is no longer automatically included in *The White Book Service* (for new subscribers). New subscribers may order the Forms Volume separately. However, all subscribers will continue to be updated with the latest forms by way of receiving the Forms

Release. We do ask that you keep your Forms Volume from one year to the next and update by way of filing the releases supplied, particularly as we cross–refer from the text of the CPR to forms in the Forms Volume and Forms CD. We avoid the duplication of forms in both the main volumes and the Forms Volume. This includes Practice Direction forms.

The Forms Release is nominally published three times a year. We will not publish a paper forms release with the two supplements unless the number of new or amended forms released by the MOJ demands it (we will continue to release the Forms CD as normal). You will find a paper forms release released with the main volumes, which is the twenty–fifth release.

Forms on CD–ROM and Adobe forms

Electronic forms on the Forms and the White Book CDs are available in two formats—RTF/Word and PDF.

As a basic requirement, all 600–odd court forms and notes are available in RTF/Word format. All are also available as interactive PDFs, many of which are able to be edited and saved using Adobe functionality. Please refer to the accompanying Quick Reference Card for full details.

Email alerters

You may wish to sign up to receive our Forms email alerter service. An email notice is sent to you when new court forms are published by the Court Service. You can also download forms via our website: **http://www.sweetandmaxwell.co.uk/whitebook**. Click on "White Book Updating Service", enter the password: **WB2010** and click on "What's New".

You may also wish to sign up to receive our email alerter service to notify you of changes to the Civil Procedure Rules as they are introduced by Statutory Instrument and as the changes come into force. This service is also available via **http://www.sweetandmaxwell.co.uk/whitebook**.

How to use Civil Procedure 2010

This is a Special Supplement to *Civil Procedure* 2010. Updating information is referenced to the relevant paragraph in the Main Volumes. The instructions in italics explain how the added material relates to the Main Volumes.

As ever, we have endeavoured to ensure that the content of *The White Book* is presented logically. The Civil Procedure Rules are reproduced in bold type to ensure they are easily distinguished from editorial comment and Practice Directions. Notes have been added to provide a full record of the changes to the Civil Procedure Rules. CPR Part numbers have been added to the thumb tabs at the side of each page.

Please refer to your User Guide which walks you through the navigational features and various components of *The White Book*

Service, including the new cross–references to the additional content online and on CD.

Volume 1

The Civil Procedure Rules and Practice Directions (including Schs 1 and 2 containing those RSC and CCR still in force) are contained in Vol.1 with the following exceptions:

– *CPR on Specialist lists*—CPR Pts 58–63 (dealing with the Commercial Court, the Mercantile Courts, the Technology and Construction Court, Admiralty Claims and Arbitrations, and Patents and Other Intellectual Property Claims) are set out in Vol.2, Section 2.

– *CPR Pt 49—Specialist proceedings*—the proceedings dealt with under the Practice Direction to Pt 49 (Proceedings under the Companies Acts) are set out in Vol.2, Section 2.

Miscellaneous Practice Directions, Pre–Action Protocols, procedural guides and a guide to time limits are also reproduced in Vol.1.

Volume 2

The main elements of Vol.2 are the specialist areas of practice and procedure: the specialist lists dealt with by CPR Pts 58–63 and the specialist proceedings under CPR Pt 49, other specialist proceedings (e.g. Housing and Consumer) and procedural legislation. Volume 2 also includes Litigation and Procedural Topics such as Interim Remedies and Alternative Dispute Resolution.

A quick guide to finding key materials is set out below. See the separate User Guide for further information.

How to find ...

... CPR Rules and Supplementary Practice Directions (Vol.1, Section A)

The Civil Procedure Rules and Practice Directions are contained in Section A, which adopts the following paragraph system.

Part 3, r.1	para.**3.1**
Commentary to Part 3, r.1	para.3.1.**1**, (3.1.**2** etc.)
Practice Direction supplementing Part 3	para.3**PD**.1
Second Practice Direction supplementing Part 3	para.3**B**PD.1

The paragraph numbers appear at the top outside corner of each page.

... Rules of the Supreme Court, County Court Rules and Supplementary Practice Directions

Section A also contains the re–enacted Rules of the Supreme Court and County Court Rules, with all supplementary Practice Directions. The following paragraph system is used:

RSC Order 52, r.1	para.**sc**52.1
Commentary to RSC Order 52.1	para.sc52.1.**1**, (sc52.1.**2** etc.)
Practice Direction supplementing Order 52	para.sc**pd**52.1
CCR Order 1, r.6	para.**cc**1.6
Commentary to CCR Order 1, r.6	para.cc1.6.**1**

... Miscellaneous Practice Direction (Vol.1, Section B)
Practice Directions which are not supplementary to a rule (e.g. the Practice Direction on Insolvency Proceedings) are contained in Section B, which adopts the following paragraph system.

Practice Direction Insolvency Proceedings, etc.	para.B1–001

... Pre–Action Protocols (Vol.1, Section C)
The Pre–Action Protocols are contained in Section C, which adopts the following paragraph system:

Practice Direction—Protocols	para.C**0**–001
Pre–Action Protocol for Personal Injury Claims	para.C**1**–001

... Chancery Guide
The Chancery Guide Appears in Section 1 of Vol.2 and is numbered para.1–1 onwards.

... Specialist Practice Directions under CPR Parts 58–63 and Specialist Court Guides, Applications under the Companies Act
Specialist Proceedings under CPR Parts 58–63 and Specialist Court Guides, Applications under the Companies Act appear in Section 2 of Vol.2 as follows:

CPR 58	Commercial Court
CPR 59	Mercantile Courts
CPR 60	Technology and Construction Courts
CPR 61	Admiralty Claims
CPR 62	Arbitration Claims
CPR 63	Patents and other Intellectual Property Claims
Practice Direction to CPR 49	Applications Under the Companies Act

... Forms
The forms are located in the Civil Procedure Forms Volume and on the Forms CD.

... Litigation and Procedural Topics
These are located at the end of Vol.2 in Sections 11 to 15.

Service Elements

The White Book Service allows you to choose a customised product to suit your requirements.

Civil Procedure CD and Print Service
Annual subscription includes:
CD (includes all content in Vols 1 and 2 and the Forms Volume and additional research materials)
Civil Procedure 2010 Vol.1
Civil Procedure 2010 Vol.2
Civil Procedure Forms Updates
Civil Procedure Forms Volume (on request to new subscribers)
Cumulative paper supplements

Civil Procedure News (10 issues a year)
Internet–based primary law updating
Forms email Alerter Service
Rules email Alerter Service
Subscription price: £539 plus VAT

Civil Procedure Volumes 1 and 2
Annual subscription includes:
Civil Procedure 2010 Vol.1
Civil Procedure 2010 Vol.2
Civil Procedure Forms CD
Civil Procedure Forms Updates
Civil Procedure Forms Volume (on request to new subscribers)
Cumulative paper supplements
Civil Procedure News (10 issues a year)
Internet–based primary law updating
Forms email Alerter Service
Rules email Alerter Service
Subscription price: £465 plus VAT

Civil Procedure Volume 1
Annual subscription includes:
Civil Procedure 2010 Vol.1
Civil Procedure Forms CD
Civil Procedure Forms Updates
Civil Procedure Forms Volume (on request to new subscribers)
Cumulative paper supplements
Civil Procedure News (10 issues a year)
Internet–based primary law updating
Forms email Alerter Service
Rules email Alerter Service
Subscription price: £360 plus VAT

White Book on Westlaw UK

Please contact our Westlaw UK helpdesk for further information on 0800 028 2200.

Customer Services

If you have a query relating to your subscription or you wish to purchase extra copies of Civil Procedure 2010, please call our Customer Services team on:

UK direct customers: 0845 600 9355

UK trade customers: 0845 082 1032

International customers: +44 (0) 1264 388560

Or you can write to:

Customer Services
Sweet & Maxwell
Freepost
PO Box 2000
Andover
SP10 9AH

United Kingdom
Website: *http://www.sweetandmaxwell.co.uk*
Email: *sweetandmaxwell.customer.services@thomson.com*

Comments and feedback

We are always pleased to receive comments and suggestions from customers. Address correspondence to: Publishing Editor, The White Book Service, Sweet & Maxwell, 100 Avenue Road, London, NW3 3PF or email *whitebook@sweetandmaxwell.co.uk*

The White Book Team

March 2010

TABLE OF STATUTES

VOLUME 1

CIVIL PROCEDURE RULES

SECTION A

CIVIL PROCEDURE RULES 1998

PART 8

ALTERNATIVE PROCEDURE FOR CLAIMS

Contents **8.0.1**

In the table of contents, the following entry has been added:

RTA Protocol Practice Direction (PD 8B)

Add new paragraph 8.0.4.2:

Practice Direction 8B (Pre-Action Protocol for Low Value Personal Injury Claims in **8.0.4.2** Road Traffic Accidents—Stage 3 Procedure) supplements r.8.1(6). The Editorial Introduction inserted at the beginning of the text of the practice direction gives an explanation of its purposes principal effects (see para.8BPD.0 below). Practice Direction 8B came into effect on April 30, 2010, and relates to CPR Pt 36 Section II and Pt 45 Section VI as inserted by the Civil Procedure (Amendment) Rules 2010.

Related sources

After the last bullet point, add new bullet point:

- Pre-Action Protocol for Low Value Personal Injury Claims in Road Traffic Accidents **8.0.6**

Types of claim in which Part 8 procedure may or must be followed

After the seventh paragraph, add as a new paragraph:

A claim made under the Stage 3 Procedure where the parties have followed the **8.1.1** Pre-Action Protocol for Low Value Personal Injury Claims in Road Traffic Accidents is made under Practice Direction 8B where the procedure is set out (see para.8.0.4.2 above and para.8BPD.0 below). The claim is made pursuant to Pt 8 as modified by PD 8B.

PRACTICE DIRECTION 8B—PRE-ACTION PROTOCOL FOR LOW VALUE PERSONAL INJURY CLAIMS IN ROAD TRAFFIC ACCIDENTS—STAGE 3 PROCEDURE

This Practice Direction supplements rule 8.1(6)

Editorial introduction

Add new paragraphs 8BPD.0 to 8BPD.17:

The Pre-Action Protocol for Low Value Personal Injury Claims in Road Traffic Ac- **8BPD.0** cidents ("the RTA Protocol") (see para.13–001 below) describes the behaviour the court will normally expect of the parties prior to the start of proceedings where a claimant claims damages valued at no more than £10,000 as a result of a personal injury sustained by that person in a road traffic accident (para.2.1). It applies to claims arising out of accidents occurring on or after April 30, 2010. The pre–action processes which the parties are expected to follow are set out in detail in the Protocol and are divided into two consecutive stages, Stage 1 and Stage 2 (the second coming into play where there has been an admission of liability by the defendant under the first). Fixed costs, as provided for in CPR Pt 45, Sect.VI are recoverable by the claimant at various points during these processes, and under Stage 2 the claimant is entitled to interim payments of damages. (For further commentary on the RTA Protocol, see para.C13A–001 below.)

In relation to the type of claim to which it relates, the RTA Protocol supplants the Pre–Action Protocol for Personal Injury Claims. A claimant wishing to start court proceedings for a claim of the type covered by the RTA Protocol would normally start those proceedings by issuing a claim form under CPR Pt 7, and the Protocol provides that, in various circumstances, before the parties have exhausted the processes set out therein, the claimant may start proceedings in this way (see paras 7.19, 7.21, 7.33, 7.39, 7.51 and 7.66). However the RTA Protocol further provides that, where the parties have followed the negotiating processes set out therein but are unable to agree the amount of damages payable at the end of Stage 2, court proceedings to determine the amount of damages should be started, not under Pt 7, but "under Part 8 in accordance with Practice Direction 8B". In the RTA Protocol and in Practice Direction 8B, this modified Pt 8 procedure is referred to as "the Stage 3 Procedure". The Stage 3 Procedure builds on the RTA Protocol processes. In various ways the procedure restricts the issues that can be contested and the evidence that may be adduced, in effect treating steps taken by the parties during the Stage 1 and (particularly) the Stage 2 processes as steps that might otherwise have been taken during the post–issue and pre–trial stages of a claim started under Pt 7.

The Stage 3 Procedure is also to be followed where a claim is made by a child and the parties have reached a settlement at the end of Stage 2 of the RTA Protocol and the approval of the court is required in relation to the settlement in accordance with r.21.10(2). (The RTA Protocol does not apply where the claimant or defendant is a protected party as defined in r.21.2(d).)

Paragraph 4.1 of Practice Direction 8B states that the court may "at any stage" order a claim that has been started under Pt 7 to continue under the Pt 8 procedure as modified by that Practice Direction. In the circumstances provided for in para.7.2 the court may order that a claim started under the Stage 3 procedure should be continued under Pt 7, and where, in the circumstances provided for in para.9.1, the defendant opposes the claim, the court will dismiss the claim, leaving the claimant with the option of starting proceedings under Pt 7.

The RTA Protocol and Practice Direction 8B recognise that compliance with the Protocol's terms may not be possible before the expiry of the limitation period relevant to the claimant's claim (generally three years from the date of accident). It is provided (in para.5.7 of the Protocol and in para.16 of PD 8B) that, in this event, the claimant may start court proceedings and apply to the court for an order to stay the proceedings "while the parties take steps to follow this Protocol" (see further commentary in para.8BPD.16.1 below).

The RTA Protocol differs in significant respects from the other Pre–Action Protocols. The fact that it is linked (as explained above) to a bespoke court procedure for claims to which it applies is but one example. Another is that, where at the end of Stage 2 the parties are unable to agree the amount of damages payable, and the prospect of proceedings being started under the Stage 3 procedure looms, the Protocol provides that defendants must pay the claimant (except where the claimant is a child) their final offer of damages together with disbursements (reasonable if not agreed) and the fixed costs payable under the Protocol provisions. (Such payment is referred to as "a non–settlement payment"; see para.7.61.)

A claim under Practice Direction 8B must be started in a county court. The defendant is required to acknowledge service in a form specially designed for that purpose (Form **N210B**) (para.8.1). The claim will not be allocated to a case management track; Parts 26 to 29 do not apply (para.17.1). Normally the claim will be heard by a district judge (para.1.2). A determination of the claim may be made on paper or at "a Stage 3 hearing" (para.11.1).

In court proceedings started under the Stage 3 procedure the rules in Sect.II of CPR Pt 36 (Offers to Settle) apply. Rule 36.21 states the costs consequences of an "RTA Protocol offer". An admission made by a party during the RTA Protocol processes is a pre–action admission for the purposes of CPR Pt 14 (Admissions). Rule 14.1B deals with the circumstances in which such an admission may be withdrawn.

Court proceedings started under the Stage 3 procedure are subject to the fixed costs regime contained in Sect.VI of Pt 45 (Fixed Costs) (see r.45.27(1)). The costs allowed are the fixed costs in r.45.29, disbursements in r.45.30, and a success fee calculated in accordance with r.45.31.

CPR practice directions supplement or complement the rules in CPR Parts. With Practice Direction 8B, the position is reversed. Rule 14.1B, Sect.II of CPR Pt 36 (Offers to Settle), and Sect.VI of Pt 45 (Fixed Costs) were inserted in the CPR (by the Civil Procedure (Amendment) Rules 2010) enacting rules integral to the Stage 3 Procedure set out in the Practice Direction and, indeed, having no other effects except in relation to that procedure.

General

1.1 This Practice Direction sets out the procedure ("the Stage 3 Procedure") for a claim where— **8BPD.1**

(1) the parties—

(a) have followed the Pre-Action Protocol for Low Value Personal Injury Claims in Road Traffic Accidents ("the RTA Protocol"); but

(b) are unable to agree the amount of damages payable at the end of Stage 2 of the RTA Protocol;

(2) (a) the claimant is a child;

(b) a settlement has been agreed by the parties at the end of Stage 2 of the RTA Protocol; and

(c) the approval of the court is required in relation to the settlement in accordance with rule 21.10(2);

(3) compliance with the RTA Protocol is not possible before the expiry of a limitation period and proceedings are started in accordance with paragraph 16 of this Practice Direction.

1.2 A claim under this practice direction must be started in a county court and will normally be heard by a district judge.

Note

A claim is started (or proceedings are started) by the issue of a claim form, not (as para.1.2 states) "under this practice direction", but more accurately (as CPR rules related to such a claim state) "under Part 8 in accordance with Practice Direction 8B" (see e.g. r.36.16(2) and r.45.27(1)). Paragraph 2.1 speaks of a claim "made under the Part 8 procedure as modified by this Practice Direction". In legal discourse the procedure is likely to be called, simply, "the Stage 3 Procedure" (as in paras 7.2, 8.3 and 8.4 of PD 8B), provided it is remembered that the procedure may come into play in circumstances other than where the parties have engaged in the RTA Protocol processes (see para.4.1 of PD 8B). Under the RTA Protocol, "claim" means a claim, prior to the start of proceedings, for payment of damages under the process set out in that Protocol (para.1.1(1)). Where a claim is made, not only by a child (as para.1.1(2) envisages), but also against a child, no settlement is valid without the approval of the court (r.21.10(1)). **8BPD.1.1**

Modification of Part 8

2.1 The claim is made under the Part 8 procedure as modified by this practice direction and subject to paragraph 2.2. **8BPD.2**

2.2 The claim will be determined by the court on the contents of the Court Proceedings Pack. The following rules do not apply to an application under this Practice Direction—

(1) rule 8.2A (issue of a claim form without naming defendants);

(2) rule 8.3 (acknowledgment of service);

(3) rule 8.5 (filing and serving witness evidence);

(4) rule 8.6 (evidence—general);

(5) rule 8.7 (Part 20 claims);

(6) rule 8.8 (procedure where defendant objects to use of the Part 8 procedure); and

(7) rule 8.9(c).

Note

8BPD.2.1 Where the parties do not reach agreement in Stage 2 of the RTA Protocol process, the claimant must send the Court Proceedings Pack (Part A and Part B) to the defendant (ibid para.7.55). Generally, where the Pt 8 procedure is followed, the claim is treated as allocated to the multi–track (r.8.9(c)). Obviously, this would be inappropriate for proceedings to which PD 8B applies and for which the procedures in it are intended. Under the CPR, "application" is a term of art, and an application is made on an application notice. Where a claim is made under Pt 8 as modified by PD 8B, it is likely that the parties will make applications to the court in the proceedings, but that would not be "an application under this Practice Direction" within para.2.2.

Definitions

8BPD.3 **3.1** References to 'the Court Proceedings Pack (Part A) Form', 'the Court Proceedings Pack (Part B) Form' and 'the CNF Response Form' are references to the forms used in the RTA Protocol.

3.2 "RTA Protocol offer" has the meaning given in rule 36.17.

3.3 "Settlement hearing" means a hearing where the court considers a settlement agreed between the parties (whether before or after proceedings have started) and the claimant is a child.

3.4 "Stage 3 hearing" means a final hearing to determine the amount of damages that remain in dispute between the parties.

Note

8BPD.3.1 As to contents of the Pack, see para.7.49 et seq of the RTA Protocol. The expression "RTA Protocol offer" is not a term of art within the RTA Protocol, and its only use in PD 8B is in para.10.1 (Withdrawal of the RTA Protocol offer). Where a judgment is given in proceedings under the Stage 3 procedure set out in PD 8B, an RTA Protocol offer will have the costs consequences set out in r.36.21, and it is in that context that the meaning of the expression as given in r.36.17 (Form and content of RTA Protocol offer) becomes important. For further information on the nature of such offers and the possible consequences, see commentary following r.39.21.

Types of claim in which this modified Part 8 procedure may be followed

8BPD.4 **4.1** The court may at any stage order a claim that has been started under Part 7 to continue under the Part 8 procedure as modified by this Practice Direction.

Note

8BPD.4.1 The heading to this paragraph is misleading. In various circumstances, a claim may no longer continue under the RTA Protocol processes and proceedings may be started under Pt 7. (Express references in the RTA Protocol to the starting of proceedings under Pt 7 are in paras 7.19, 7,21, 7,33, 7.39, 7.51 and 7.66.) Claims which no longer continue under the Protocol cannot subsequently re–enter the process (para.5.10). In terms, para.4.1 (by providing that the court "may at any stage order a claim") appears to apply to any claim that has been started under Pt 7 and in any circumstances.

The costs provisions in Sect.VI of Pt 45 apply to claims that have been started, or should have been started, under PD 8B (see r.45.27(1)), and, presumably, to claims that had been started under Pt 7 but are continued under the Pt 8 procedure as modified by this Practice Direction by an order made under this paragraph.

An application to the court to determine the amount of damages

8BPD.5 **5.1** An application to the court to determine the amount of damages must be started by a claim form.

5.2 The claim form must state—

(1) that the claimant has followed the procedure set out in the RTA Protocol;

(2) the date when the Court Proceedings Pack (Part A and Part B) Form was sent to the defendant. (This provision does not apply where the claimant is a child and the application is for a settlement hearing);

(3) whether the claimant wants the claim to be determined by the court on the papers (except where a party is a child) or at a Stage 3 hearing;

(4) where the claimant seeks a settlement hearing or Stage 3 hearing, the dates which the claimant requests should be avoided; and

(5) the value of the claim.

Note

Paragraphs 5.1 to 8.4 clearly apply where the Stage 3 Procedure has been invoked for a claim in which the parties have followed the RTA Protocol processes, but were unable to agree the amount of damages payable at the end of Stage 2 of those processes. A claim made under the Stage 3 procedure in those circumstances is aptly described as "an application to the court to determine the amount of damages" (para.5.1). However, that description is not apt where the circumstances are that the claimant is a child and the Stage 3 procedure applies for the purpose of obtaining the court's approval of a settlement agreed by the parties during Stage 1 or Stage 2 of the Protocol processes (r.21.10(2)). (In other circumstances, application for approval is made under r.21.10, using the procedure set out in Pt 8.) Nevertheless, it would seem that the procedures set out in paras 5.1. to 8.5 apply as far as may be to an application for approval made in this way (see in particular para.6.5). RTA Protocol offers must be set out in Court Proceedings Pack (Part B) Form. The fixing of the date on which the Form was sent to the defendant (para.5.2(2)) is important for the purposes of determining the costs consequences following judgment under the Stage 3 Procedure of an RTA Protocol offer and calculating interest thereon (see further rr.36.18 and 36.21). **8BPD.5.1**

Filing and serving written evidence

6.1 The claimant must file with the claim form— **8BPD.6**

(1) the Court Proceedings Pack (Part A) Form;

(2) the Court Proceedings Pack (Part B) Form (the claimant and defendant's final offers) in a sealed envelope. (This provision does not apply where the claimant is a child and the application is for a settlement hearing);

(3) copies of medical reports;

(4) evidence of special damages;

(5) evidence of disbursements (for example the cost of any medical report) in accordance with rule 45.30(2); and

(6) any notice of funding.

6.2 The filing of the claim form and documents set out in paragraph 6.1 represent the start of Stage 3 for the purposes of fixed costs.

6.3 Subject to paragraph 6.5 the claimant must only file those documents in paragraph 6.1 where they have already been sent to the defendant under the RTA Protocol.

6.4 The claimant's evidence as set out in paragraph 6.1 must be served on the defendant with the claim form.

6.5 Where the claimant is a child the claimant must also provide to the court the following in relation to a settlement made before or after the start of proceedings—

(1) the draft consent order;

(2) the advice by counsel, solicitor or other legal representative on the amount of damages; and

(3) a statement verified by a statement of truth signed by the litigation friend which confirms whether the child has recovered in accordance with the prognosis and whether there are any continuing symptoms. This statement will enable the court to decide whether to order the child to attend the settlement hearing.

6.6 Where the defendant is uninsured and the Motor Insurers' Bureau ("MIB") or its agents have consented in the CNF Response Form to the MIB being joined as a defendant, the claimant must name the MIB as the second defendant and must also provide to the court a copy of the CNF Response Form completed by or on behalf of the MIB.

6.7 Where this Practice Direction requires a step to be taken by the defendant, it will be sufficient for this step to be taken by the MIB.

Note

8BPD.6.1 Where the parties do not reach an agreement under Stage 2 of the RTA Protocol processes as to the amount of damages, the claimant must send the Court Proceedings Pack (Part A and Part B) Form, referred to in para.6.1(1) and (2), to the defendant (para.7.55). The Pack must contain supporting comments from both parties on disputed heads of damages (ibid). Whether other documents of the type referred to in para.6.1 have been sent to the defendant will depend on the circumstances of the case. The important point is that they cannot be filed unless they have been so sent, and sent "under the RTA Protocol".

Paragraph 6.5 applies where the claimant is a child and a settlement has been agreed by the parties "before or after the start of proceedings". The provision clearly applies where a settlement was agreed by the parties at the end of Stage 2 of the RTA Protocol, and the Stage 3 Procedure was invoked for the purposes of obtaining the court's approval of the settlement. But it may also apply where that was not the case, and the procedure was invoked because the parties were unable to reach agreement at Stage 2, but managed to do so after proceedings had been started under the Stage 3 Procedure. The material that the child claimant is required to provide for the court under para.6.5 may be contrasted with that required under Practice Direction 21 (Children and Patients) para.5.

Evidence—general

8BPD.7 **7.1** The parties may not rely upon evidence unless—

(1) it has been served in accordance with paragraph 6.4;

(2) it has been filed in accordance with paragraph 8.2 and 11.3; or

(3) (where the court considers that it cannot properly determine the claim without it), the court orders otherwise and gives directions.

7.2 Where the court considers that—

(1) further evidence must be provided by any party; and

(2) the claim is not suitable to continue under the Stage 3 Procedure,

the court will order that the claim will continue under Pt 7, allocate the claim to a track and give directions.

7.3 Where paragraph 7.2 applies the court will not allow the Stage 3 fixed costs.

Note

Paragraphs 7.1 to 7.3 demonstrate that, under the Stage 3 procedure, the material that the court will consider in determining the amount of damages is restricted. The procedure builds on the Stage 2 process. It is not designed to give the parties the opportunity to put forward new material that was not exchanged during that process. Where the defendant opposes the claim because the claimant has filed and served additional or new evidence with the claim form that had not been provided under the RTA Protocol, the court will dismiss the claim (para.9.1). The power of the court to order that the claim is not suitable to continue under the Stage 3 process is a power the court may exercise on its own initiative. **8BPD.7.1**

Acknowledgment of Service

8.1 The defendant must file and serve an acknowledgment of service in Form N210B not more than 14 days after service of the claim form. **8BPD.8**

8.2 The defendant must file and serve—

(1) with the acknowledgment of service, any notice of funding; and

(2) with the acknowledgment of service, or as soon as possible thereafter, a certificate that is in force.

('Certificate' is defined in rule 36.15(1)(e)(i).)

8.3 The acknowledgment of service must state whether the defendant—

(1) (a) contests the amount of damages claimed;

(b) contests the making of an order for damages;

(c) disputes the court's jurisdiction; or

(d) objects to the use of the Stage 3 procedure;

(2) wants the claim to be determined by the court on the papers or at a Stage 3 hearing.

8.4 Where the defendant objects to the use of the Stage 3 Procedure reasons must be give in the acknowledgment of service.

8.5 The acknowledgment of service may be signed and filed by the defendant's insurer who may give their address as the address for service.

Dismissal of the claim

9.1 Where the defendant opposes the claim because the claimant has— **8BPD.9**

(1) not followed the procedure set out in the RTA Protocol; or

(2) filed and served additional or new evidence with the claim form that had not been provided under the RTA Protocol,

the court will dismiss the claim and the claimant may start proceedings under Part 7.

(Rule 45.36 sets out the costs consequences of failing to comply with the RTA Protocol.)

Note

A dismissal of the claim under para.9.1 on the basis of the defendant's objections is a dismissal otherwise than on the merits and is, in effect, a procedural sanction (but presumably not one from which CPR r.3.9 relief may be sought), designed to ensure that claimants follow Stage 2 of the RTA Protocol processes conscientiously. The **8BPD.9.1** alternative of starting proceedings under Pt 7 may be of no use to the claimant where the limitation period has run. See further para.8BPD.16.1 below.

Withdrawal of the RTA Protocol offer

8BPD.10 **10.1** A party may only withdraw an RTA Protocol offer after proceedings have started with the court's permission. Where the court gives permission the claim will no longer continue under the Stage 3 Procedure and the court will give directions. The court will only give permission where there is good reason for the claim not to continue under the Stage 3 Procedure.

Note

8BPD.10.1 As to RTA Protocol offers, see commentary in CPR Pt 36 Sect.II, especially on rr.36.17 and 36.18.

Consideration of the claim

8BPD.11 **11.1** The court will order that damages are to be assessed—

(1) on the papers; or

(2) at a Stage 3 hearing where—

(a) the claimant so requests on the claim form;

(b) the defendant so requests in the acknowledgment of service (Form N210B); or

(c) the court so orders,

and on a date determined by the court.

11.2 The court will give the parties at least 21 days notice of the date of the determination on the papers or the date of the Stage 3 hearing.

11.3 Where further deductible amounts have accrued since the final offer was made by both parties in the Court Proceedings Pack (Part B) Form, the defendant must file an up to date certificate at least 5 days before the date of a determination on the papers.

('Deductible amount' is defined in rule 36.15(1)(d).)

11.4 Where the claim is determined on the papers the court will give reasons for its decision in the judgment.

Settlement at Stage 2 where the claimant is a child

8BPD.12 **12.1** Paragraphs 12.2 to 12.5 apply where—

(1) the claimant is a child;

(2) there is a settlement at Stage 2 of the RTA Protocol; and

(3) an application is made to the court to approve the settlement.

12.2 Where the settlement is approved at the settlement hearing the court will order the costs to be paid in accordance with rule 45.33(2).

12.3 Where the settlement is not approved at the first settlement hearing and the court orders a second settlement hearing at which the settlement is approved, the court will order the costs to be paid in accordance with rule 45.33(4) to (6).

12.4 Where the settlement is not approved at the first settlement hearing and the court orders that the claim is not suitable to be determined under the Stage 3 Procedure, the court will order costs to be paid in accordance with rule 45.35 and will give directions.

12.5 Where the settlement is not approved at the second settlement hearing the claim will no longer continue under the Stage 3 Procedure and the court will give directions.

Settlement at Stage 3 where the claimant is a child

13.1 Paragraphs 13.2 and 13.3 apply where— **8BPD.13**

(1) the claimant is a child;

(2) there is a settlement after proceedings have started under the Stage 3 Procedure; and

(3) an application is made to the court to approve the settlement.

13.2 Where the settlement is approved at the settlement hearing the court will order the costs to be paid in accordance with rule 45.34(2).

13.3 Where the settlement is not approved at the settlement hearing the court will order the claim to proceed to a Stage 3 hearing.

Adjournment

14.1 Where the court adjourns a settlement hearing or a Stage 3 hearing it may, in its discretion, order the costs to be paid in accordance with rule 45.39. **8BPD.14**

Appeals—determination on the papers

15.1 The court will not consider an application to set aside a judgment made after a determination on the papers. The judgment will state the appeal court to which an appeal lies. **8BPD.15**

Limitation

16.1 Where compliance with the RTA Protocol is not possible before the expiry of a limitation period the claimant may start proceedings in accordance with paragraph 16.2. **8BPD.16**

16.2 The claimant must—

(1) start proceedings under this Practice Direction; and

(2) state on the claim form that—

(a) the claim is for damages; and

(b) a stay of proceedings is sought in order to comply with the RTA Protocol.

16.3 The claimant must send to the defendant the claim form together with the order imposing the stay.

16.4 Where a claim is made under paragraph 16.1 the provisions in this Practice Direction, except paragraphs 1.2, 2.1, 2,2 and 16.1 to 16.6, are disapplied.

16.5 Where—

(1) a stay is granted by the court;

(2) the parties have complied with the RTA Protocol; and

(3) the claimant wishes to start the Stage 3 Procedure,

the claimant must make an application to the court to lift the stay and request directions.

16.6 Where the court orders that the stay be lifted—

(1) the provisions of this Practice Direction will apply; and

(2) the claimant must—

(a) amend the claim form in accordance with paragraph 5.2; and

(b) file the documents in paragraph 6.1.

16.7 Where, during Stage 1 or Stage 2 of the RTA Protocol—

(1) the claim no longer continues under that Protocol; and

(2) the claimant wishes to start proceedings under Part 7,

the claimant must make an application to the court to lift the stay and request directions.

Note

8BPD.16.1 The Limitation Act 1980 s.11 states that an action in respect of personal injuries "shall not be brought" after the expiration of the period of three years from the date on which the cause of action accrued or the date of knowledge (if later) of the person injured. Once the limitation period is in relation to a cause of action to which the RTA Protocol applies starts to run, nothing can stop it. According to CPR r.7.2, "proceedings are started" when the court issues a claim form at the request of the claimant. A claim form is issued on the date entered on the form by the court (r.7.2(2)). Where that date is after the expiration of the three–year period the action falls foul of s.11; where it is not, it does not. (In the former instance, the defendant may plead limitation. If that plea is successful, the claimant's cause of action is not extinguished; but encounters a permanent procedural bar preventing it from being pursued.) CPR r.7.5 states that, where (as will normally be the case where an action is brought in respect of personal injuries) the claim form is to be served within the jurisdiction, the "step required" appropriate to the method of service must be completed before 12.00 midnight on the calendar day four months after the date of issue of the claim form. This time limit may be varied by the written agreement of the parties (unless the court orders otherwise) (r.2.11), and, in restricted circumstances, may be extended by order of the court (r.7.6).

The RTA Protocol describes the behaviour the court will normally expect of the parties "prior to the start of proceedings" (para.2.1). The Protocol and Practice Direction 8B anticipate that, in a given case, the compliance by the parties with the Protocol processes may not be possible before the expiry of the primary limitation period, and concede (they could hardly do otherwise) that the claimant, in order to ensure that the action is brought within that period, may have to "start proceedings" before those processes have been commenced or completed. Paragraph 16.2 of PD 8B states that a claimant taking this step must "start proceedings under this Practice Direction" (para.16.2(1)). That is misleading (and neither para.1.1(3) of PD 8B nor para.5.8 of the Protocol do not do much better in this respect) as it suggests that, in these circumstances, proceedings are started under the Stage 3 Procedure. It would be more accurate to say that, where proceedings are started for limitation protection purposes, they are started "under Part 8 in accordance with Practice Direction 8B" (see para.8BPD.1.1 above), and specifically in accordance with para.16 (this is reinforced by para.16.4, disapplying most of PD 8B). The procedure stands apart from the Stage 3 procedure and has its effects before that procedure comes into play.

A court order staying proceedings may be granted in various circumstances and for various purposes and may contain terms distinguishing between those procedural steps that the parties may or may not take, or should or should not take, whilst the stay subsists. Paragraph 16.2 is inelegant. It states that, where a claimant seeks a stay what is sought is a stay "in order to comply with the RTA Protocol". Presumably what is meant is that a stay granted in these circumstances is a stay generally, preventing either party from taking a further step in the proceedings without the permission of the court. The principal significance of such an order in this context is that it suspends the normal CPR procedures that would follow upon the issue of a claim form (in particular, those dealing with the service by the claimant of the claim form and the particulars of claim in accordance with rr.7.4 and 7.5). For obvious reasons, it is expressly provided that a claimant starting proceedings under para.16.2 must immediately notify the defendant accordingly (para.16.3). Where a claimant takes advantage of para.16.2, proceedings are started by the issue of a claim form and any question as to whether the action has been brought before the expiry of the limitation period that might arise subsequently will fall to be determined on the basis that it was brought on the date of issue. The starting of proceedings under para.16.2 and the imposing of a stay on those proceedings do not have the effect of suspending the running of the limitation period.

By r.16.2, the claimant is required to "state on the claim form that ... a stay of proceedings is sought". In effect, by issuing the claim form the claimant starts the proceedings and makes an application without notice but on notice for a stay. (The stay application is not a pre–action application.)

The terms of para.16.2 are permissive, not mandatory. But a claimant anticipating that compliance with the RTA Protocol was not possible before the expiry of the limitation period would be wise to take advantage of it. The court fees payable "where proceedings are started as a result of a limitation period that is about to expire" is a disbursement recoverable by the claimant (r.45.30(2)(d)).

Where a stay has been granted and, subsequently, the claimant wishes "to start the Stage 3 Procedure", the parties having complied with the RTA Protocol since the stay was granted, his proceedings are already on foot and there is no need for him to issue a claim form, but he must amend his claim form (issued for the purpose of obtaining the stay) so that it complies with para.5.2 (see paras 16.5 and 16.6 and RTA Protocol para.5.8). If the limitation period has expired in the period since the stay was granted, the claimant is not exposed to a limitation defence (it is assumed that such amendment introduces no new cause of action). Paragraph 16.7 is odd. It assumes circumstances (which may arise readily enough) in which a claimant has a claim falling within the scope of the RTA Protocol but which no longer continues under it, leaving him with the prospect of having to launch proceedings under Pt 7 in order to assert his claim. It is not obvious why it should be assumed that in these circumstances the lifting of the stay on the Pt 8 proceedings should be a prerequisite for that. The Pt 7 proceedings will be fresh proceedings, and almost certainly for a cause of action now exposed to a limitation defence. However, in these circumstances, provided after the stay was imposed on his Pt 8 proceedings the claimant had complied conscientiously with the RTA Protocol processes until his claim no longer continued under those processes, it is highly unlikely that the defendant would be able to resist an application by the claimant under s.33 of the 1980 Act to disapply s.11 to enable him to pursue those fresh (Pt 7) proceedings, should the defendant put him in the position where he had to make it (in itself an unlikely event).

Modification to the general rules

17.1 The claim will not be allocated to a track. Parts 26 to 29 do not apply. **8BPD.17**

PART 14

ADMISSIONS

Editorial introduction

Add at end:

Rule 14.1B applies to pre–action admissions made in a case to which the Pre–Action Protocol for Low Value Personal Injury Claims in Road Traffic Accidents applies; see para.C13A–001 below. **14.0.2**

Admissions made under the RTA Protocol

Add new rule 14.1B:

14.1B—(1) This rule applies to a pre–action admission made in a case to which the Pre–Action Protocol for Low Value Personal Injury Claims in Road Traffic Accidents ("the RTA Protocol") applies. **14.1B**

(2) The defendant may, by giving notice in writing withdraw an admission of causation—

- **(a) before commencement of proceedings—**
  - **(i) during the initial consideration period (or any extension to that period) as defined in the RTA Protocol; or**
  - **(ii) at any time if the person to whom the admission was made agrees; or**

(b) after commencement of proceedings—

(i) if all the parties to the proceedings consent; or

(ii) with the permission of the court.

(3) The defendant may, by giving notice in writing withdraw any other pre–action admission after commencement of proceedings—

(a) if all the parties to the proceedings consent; or

(b) with the permission of the court.

(4) An application under rule 14.1B(2)(b)(ii) or (3)(b) to withdraw a pre–action admission must be made in accordance with Part 23.

Effect of rule

Add new paragraph 14.1B.1:

14.1B.1 The Pre–Action Protocol for Low Value Personal Injury Claims in Road Traffic Accidents (RTA Protocol) describes the behaviour the court will normally expect of the parties prior to the start of proceedings where a claimant claims damages valued at no more than £10,000 as a result of a personal injury sustained by that person in a road traffic accident (see para.C13A–001 below). Where the parties exhaust the Stage 1 and Stage 2 processes prescribed by that Protocol, which provides opportunities for the defendant to make admissions, without being able to reach agreement on quantum, the claimant may pursue the claim by commencing court proceedings under the Stage 3 Procedure as set out in Practice Direction 8B. In certain circumstances, the claimant may choose not to continue under the Protocol processes and may start court proceedings under Part 7. (On these matters, see commentary in para.8BPD.0 above.) Rule 14.1B regulates the circumstances in which a defendant may be permitted to withdraw, either before or after the commencement of court proceedings an admission made under Stage 1 and Stage 2 of the RTA Protocol processes. The rule is concerned with the withdrawal of admissions made by defendants, and draws a distinction between admissions of causation and other admissions (which may include admissions of liability). The "initial consideration period" is the period of 15 days which, according to para.7.28 of the RTA Protocol, the defendant has for consideration of the Stage 2 Settlement Pack sent to him by the claimant. Rule 14.1B draws a distinction between the withdrawal of admissions before, and after, the "commencement of proceedings". In this context, "proceedings" obviously includes proceedings started under the Stage 3 Procedure, but it also includes proceedings commenced under Part 7. As is explained in commentary on Practice Direction 8B, provisions in that practice direction and in the RTA Protocol state that, in the case of a claim to which the Protocol applies, a claimant may start proceedings under Part 8 where compliance by the parties with the Protocol may not be possible before the expiry of the primary limitation period (see para.8BPD.16.1 above). It would seem that proceedings commenced in this way and for those purposes are not "proceedings" within the meaning of r.14.1B.

PRACTICE DIRECTION 14—ADMISSIONS

Admissions generally

In sub–paragraph 1.1(2), in the parenthesis at the end, for "£15,000" substitute:

14PD.1 the fast track limit

PART 21

CHILDREN AND PROTECTED PARTIES

Judgments and settlements

Add new paragraph at end:

21.0.5 For court approval of settlements where claimant is a child and the parties have followed the RTA Protocol processes and reached a settlement requiring the approval of the court under r.21.10(2), see para.21.10.2 below. (The RTA Protocol does not apply where the claimant or defendant is a protected party as defined in r.21.2(d).)

Compromise etc. by or on behalf of a child or protected party

In rule 21.10(3), for "Section II of Part 45" substitute:

Section II or Section VI of Part 45 **21.10**

Introduction

Add new paragraph at end:

Sections II and VI of Pt 45 (referred to in r.21.10(3)) impose fixed recoverable costs regimes on, respectively, certain proceedings arising from road traffic accidents, and on claims that have been started (or should have been started) under Practice Direction 8B (Pre-Action Protocol for Low Value Personal Injury Claims in Road Traffic Accidents—Stage 3 Procedure). **21.10.1**

RTA Protocol—child claimant—settlement agreed

Add new paragraph 21.10.2:

Paragraph 1.1 of Practice Direction 8B states that, where parties following the Pre-Action Protocol for Low Value Personal Injury Claims in Road Traffic Accidents ("the RTA Protocol") have agreed a settlement at the end of Stage 2 and the claimant is a child, the approval of the court required by r.21.10(2) is obtained by following the procedure set out in that Practice Direction (see para.8BPD.1 above), in particular paras 6.5 and paras 12.3 to 12.5. The Practice Direction also deals with the situation where parties have been unable to agree a settlement at the end of Stage 2, and the claimant has started court proceedings under the Stage 3 Procedure and settlement is reached in those proceedings (see paras 6.5 and paras 13.1 to 13.3). (The RTA Protocol does not apply where the claimant or defendant is a protected party as defined in r.21.2(d).) **21.10.2**

PART 27

THE SMALL CLAIMS TRACK

Costs on the small claims track

Add at end of rule 27.14(2):

(h) the Stage 1 and, where relevant, the Stage 2 fixed costs in rule 45.29 where— **27.14**

- **(i) the claim was within the scope of the Pre-Action Protocol for Low Value Personal Injury Claims in Road Traffic Accidents ("the RTA Protocol");**
- **(ii) the claimant reasonably believed that the claim was valued at more than the small claims track limit in accordance with paragraph 4.1(4) of the RTA Protocol; and**
- **(iii) the defendant admitted liability under the process set out in the RTA Protocol; but**
- **(iv) the defendant did not pay those Stage 1 and, where relevant, Stage 2 fixed costs.**

RTA Protocol Stage 1 fixed costs (r.27.14(2)(h))

Add new paragraph 27.14.6:

The Pre-Action Protocol for Low Value Personal Injury Claims in Road Traffic Accidents describes the processes which the court will normally expect parties to follow prior to the start of proceedings where a claimant claims damages valued at no more than £10,000 as a result of personal injury sustained by that person in a road traffic ac- **27.14.6** cident and, if proceedings were started for the claim, the small claims track would not be the normal track for that claim (para.4.1). The small claims track is not the normal track where the value of any claim for damages for personal injuries (defined as compensation for pain, suffering and loss of amenity) is more than £1,000 (r.26.6). Paragraph 6.18 of the RTA Protocol states that, within a particular period, the defendant must pay certain costs incurred by the claimant during the first stage of these processes. These costs are fixed by r.45.29 and are known as "Stage 1 fixed costs". Where the claimant reasonably believes that the claim is valued at between £1,000 and £10,000, but it subsequently becomes apparent that the value of the claim is less than £1,000, the claimant is entitled to the Stage 1 fixed costs (para.5.9). For a variety of reasons, a claim may cease to continue under the RTA Protocol processes. It is conceivable that a claim allocated to and proceeding on the small claims track was, before it was started, subject to those processes with the result that the claimant became entitled to Stage 1 fixed costs (and possibly to Stage 2 fixed costs). By para.(h) of r.27.14(2) the court is given power to order that Stage 1 fixed costs, if they have not been paid, should be paid by the defendant. For text of RTA Protocol and commentary thereon, see paras C13A–001 and C13–001 et seq below.

PART 36

OFFERS TO SETTLE

Editorial introduction

In the first paragraph, for "Part 36 concerns offers to settle … do so comply" substitute:

36.0.2 The rules in Sect.I of Pt 36 (rr.36.1 to 36.15) are concerned with offers to settle made in accordance with the provisions therein and the consequences which follow if such offers do comply with those provisions. (As to the scope of Sect.II (rr.36.16 to 36.21), see further para.36.16.1 below).

Related sources

After the last bullet point add new bullet point:

36.0.4
- Pre–Action Protocol for Low Value Personal Injury Claims in Road Traffic Accidents

Scope of this Part

Delete rule 36.1 and substitute:

36.A1 **36.A1—(1) This Part contains rules about—**
- **(a) offers to settle; and**
- **(b) the consequences where an offer to settle is made in accordance with this Part.**

(2) Section I of this Part contains rules about offers to settle other than where Section II applies.

(3) Section II of this Part contains rules about offers to settle where the parties have followed the Pre–Action Protocol for Low Value Personal Injury Claims in Road Traffic Accidents ("the RTA Protocol") and have started proceedings under Part 8 in accordance with Practice Direction 8B.

I. Part 36 Offers to Settle

Scope of this Section

36.1 **36.1—(1) This Section does not apply to an offer to settle to which Section II of this Part applies.**

(2) Nothing in this Section prevents a party making an offer to settle in whatever way he chooses, but if the offer is not made in accordance with rule 36.2, it will not have the consequences specified in rules 36.10, 36.11 and 36.14.

(Rule 44.3 requires the court to consider an offer to settle that does not have the costs consequences set out in this Section in deciding what order to make about costs.)

Form and content of a Part 36 offer

In rule 36.2(2)(b), for "Part 36" substitute:

Section I of Part 36 36.2

Part 36 offers—general provisions

In rule 36.3(4), for "in this Part" substitute:

in this Section 36.3

II. RTA Protocol Offers to Settle

Scope of this Section

Add new paragraphs 36.16 to 36.22.1:

36.16—(1) Where this Section applies Section I does not apply. 36.16

(2) This Section applies to an offer to settle where the parties have followed the RTA Protocol and started proceedings under Part 8 in accordance with Practice Direction 8B ("the Stage 3 procedure").

(3) A reference to the "Court Proceeding Pack Form" is a reference to the form used in the RTA Protocol.

(4) Nothing in this Section prevents a party making an offer to settle in whatever way that party chooses, but if the offer is not made in accordance with this Section, it will not have any costs consequences.

Effect of rr.36.16 to 36.21

Section II (rr.36.16 to 36.21) was added to this Part by the Civil Procedure (Amendment) Rules 2010 and contains special rules about offers to settle where the parties have followed the Pre-Action Protocol for Low Value Personal Injury Claims in Road Traffic Accidents ("the RTA Protocol") (see para.C13A-001 below) and have started proceedings under the Stage 3 procedure set out in Practice Direction 8B. The RTA Protocol describes the processes which the court will normally expect parties to follow prior to the start of proceedings where a claimant claims damages valued at no more than £10,000 as a result of personal injury sustained by that person in a road traffic accident (para.4.1). Paragraph 7.55 of the RTA Protocol states that, where the parties do not reach an agreement on the amount of damages, the claimant must send the Court Proceedings Pack (Part A and Part B) Form to the defendant. That Form must contain (amongst other things) the final offer and counter offer from the Stage 2 Settlement Pack Form (ibid). Where, having followed the Stage 1 and Stage 2 processes as stipulated in the Protocol, but having not succeeded in agreeing the amount of damages payable at the end of Stage 2, the claimant may start court proceedings against the defendant under the Stage 3 Procedure as set out in Practice Direction 8B (Pre-Action Protocol for Low Value Personal Injury Claims in Road Traffic Accidents—Stage 3 Procedure) for the purpose of determining quantum. Proceedings under the Stage 3 Procedure are subject to the fixed costs regime contained in Sect.VI of Pt 45 (r.45.27). 36.16.1

Rule 36.21 is concerned with the cost consequences following judgment by the court in proceedings under the Stage 3 Procedure of offers made by the parties during their pursuit the RTA Protocol processes. (Such an offer is defined for these purposes as "an RTA Protocol offer".) Rule 36.17 reflects para.7.55 of the RTA Protocol by stating that RTA Protocol offers should be included in Part B of the Court Proceedings Pack Form (Form RTA 7), and must contain (in a sealed envelope) the final total amounts of the offers from both parties. As would be expected, it is expressly provided that the amount of any such offer must not be communicated to the court until the claim has been decided (r.36.20). Where, for the purposes of applying the provisions of r.36.21, it is necessary for the day on which an RTA Protocol offer was made to be fixed recourse is made to r.36.19. Explanations of what is meant by "the total consideration period" and "the further consideration period" in that rule are found in para.7.28 of the RTA Protocol (see further commentary following r.36.21).

Form and content of an RTA Protocol offer

36.17 **36.17—(1) An offer to settle which is made in accordance with this rule is called an RTA Protocol offer.**

(2) An RTA Protocol offer must—

(a) be set out in the Court Proceedings Pack Form (Part B); and

(b) contain the final total amount of the offer from both parties.

Court Proceedings Pack Form

36.17.1 There are several standard forms (RTA Forms) provided for use under the RTA Protocol processes; the Court Proceedings Pack Form (Part B) is RTA Form 7. For preparation by claimant of Court Proceedings Pack, including RTA Form 7, and contents thereof (including inclusion of RTA Protocol offers in sealed envelope therein), see paras 7.55 et seq of RTA Protocol. (For Protocol and commentary thereon, see paras C13A–001 and C13–001 et seq below.)

Withdrawal of RTA Protocol offer

36.17.2 A party may withdraw an RTA Protocol offer after proceedings have been started under the Stage 3 Procedure with the court's permission. Where a party does so, the claim will no longer continue under the Stage 3 Procedure and that party must apply to the court for directions (see Practice Direction 8B para.10.1). The court will only give permission where there is good reason for the claim not to continue under the Stage 3 Procedure.

Time when an RTA Protocol offer is made

36.18 **36.18 The RTA Protocol offer is deemed to be made on the first business day after the Court Proceedings Pack (Part A and Part B) Form is sent to the defendant.**

Deemed date of offer

36.18.1 A "Part 36 offer", made in accordance with Sect.I of Pt 36, is made when it is served on the offeree by the offeror (r.36.7(1)). An "RTA Protocol offer" as defined in r.36.17 is not an offer served by one party on another during Stage 2 of the RTA Protocol processes, but an offer "made using the Court Proceedings Pack Form (Part B)" (r.36.17(2)(a)). The Court Proceedings Pack Form is prepared by the claimant after the parties have failed to reach agreement under Stage 2 and should include (in Part B) the parties' final offers. Court proceedings under the Stage 3 Procedure as set out in Practice Direction 8B are started by a claim form. The claim form must (amongst other things) state the date when the Court Proceedings Pack (Part B) Form, containing the final offer and counter offcr, was sent to the defendant (para.5.2(2) of PD 8B). It would not be wholly accurate to say that a final offer is made at the time when the Form is sent by the claimant to the defendant. Rather it is recorded there after negotiations between the parties have been completed for the purposes of any court proceedings under the Stage 3 procedure as set out in Practice Direction 8B, and thereby becomes an "RTA Protocol offer". It is important for the purposes of r.36.21 (Costs consequences following judgment) (see r.36.21(2)(b) and (5)) that RTA Protocol offers should have a date, and that date is as deemed by r.36.18; that is to say, it is the first business day after the Court Proceedings that Pack (Part A and Part B) Form is sent to the defendant (the deemed date has no significance otherwise). (For the purposes of CPR Pt 6 (Service of Documents), "business day" is to be interpreted as defined in r.6.2, and the same definition applies in the RTA Protocol (see para.1.1(8)), but this expression is not defined for the purposes of Sect.II of Pt 36.)

General provisions

36.19 An RTA Protocol offer— 36.19

(a) is treated as exclusive of all interest; and

(b) has the consequences set out in this Section only in relation to the fixed costs of the Stage 3 Procedure as provided for in rule 45.29, and not in relation to the costs of any appeal from the final decision of those proceedings.

Offers and appeal costs

As is the case with a Pt 36 offer to which Sect.I of Pt 36 applies (see r.36.3(4)), an 36.19.1
RTA Protocol offer shall have the stipulated cost consequences only in relation to the proceedings in which it is made; that is to say, only in relation to the proceedings under the Stage 3 Procedure set out in PD 8B. Claims started under that procedure are subject to the fixed costs regime set out in Sect.VI of Pt 45. (The types of these fixed costs and their amounts are as stated in r.45.29.)

Where a claim is determined under the Stage 3 Procedure and an appeal is taken, the cost consequences of for the parties of the outcome of the appeal (whatever it is) may be affected by offers made by them before the appeal (r.36.3(4)).

Restrictions on disclosure of an RTA Protocol offer

36.20—(1) The amount of the RTA Protocol offer must not be communicated to the court until the claim is determined. 36.20

(2) Any other offer to settle must not be communicated to the court at all.

(3) Once the claim is determined, the court will examine the RTA Protocol offer.

Effect of rule

Where a claim proceeds under the Stage 3 procedure set out in Practice Direction 36.20.1
8B, necessarily an RTA Protocol offer will have been made and included together with any other such offers in the Court Proceedings Pack (in a sealed envelope). That fact, but not the amount of the offers, will be known to the court.

Cost consequences following judgment

36.21—(1) This rule applies where, on the determination by the court, the claimant obtains judgment against the defendant for an amount of damages that is— 36.21

(a) less than or equal to the amount of the defendant's RTA Protocol offer;

(b) more than the defendant's RTA Protocol offer but less than the claimant's RTA Protocol offer; or

(c) equal to or more than the claimant's RTA Protocol offer.

(2) Where paragraph (1)(a) applies, the court will order the claimant to pay—

(a) the fixed costs in rule 45.38; and

(b) interest on those fixed costs from the first business day after the deemed date of the RTA Protocol offer under rule 36.18.

(3) Where paragraph (1)(b) applies, the court will order the defendant to pay the fixed costs in rule 45.32.

(4) Where paragraph (1)(c) applies, the court will order the defendant to pay—

(a) interest on the whole of the damages awarded at a rate not exceeding 10% above base rate for some or all of the period starting with the date specified in rule 36.18;

(b) the fixed costs in rule 45.32; and

(c) interest on those costs at a rate not exceeding 10% above base rate.

Judgments and costs

36.21.1 For the purposes of Sect.II of Pt 36, an RTA Protocol offer is made on a date as deemed by r.36.18, it is treated as exclusive of all interest (r.36.19(a)), and has the consequences set out in this Section only in relation to the fixed costs of the Stage 3 Procedure as provided for in r.45.29 (and not in relation to the costs of any appeal from the final decision of those proceedings) (r.36.19(b)). Those provisions form the background to r.36.21. Practitioners familiar with r.36.14, which deals with the costs consequences following judgment of Pt 36 offers, will immediately recognise that r.36.21 is designed for the purpose of applying a similar regime to RTA Protocol offers. In certain respects, determining the consequences of RTA Protocol offers turns on fixing the date on which it was made. This requires recourse to r.36.18 where a date is deemed for these purposes (see further commentary following that rule).

For obvious reasons, r.36.1 proceeds on the assumptions (1) that the claimant has made an RTA Protocol offer (CO); (2) that the defendant has also made such an offer (DO); and (3) that the former is for an amount greater than the latter; and (4) that judgment has been obtained for an amount that, when contrasted with the offers, falls into one of three mutually exclusive categories; they are, (a) where the judgment is equal to or more than CO (J1), (b) where the judgment is less than J1 but is more than DO (J2), (c) where the judgment (qualified by r.36.22) is less than or equal to DO (J3). In the case of J1, the court will order (as provided by r.36.21(1)(c) and (4)) that the claimant is entitled to the fixed costs in r.45.32, and interest on those costs. (The claimant is also entitled to interest on the whole of the damages awarded (r.36.21(4)(a)). In the case of J2, the court will order (as provided by r.36.21(1)(b) and (3)) that the claimant is entitled to the fixed costs in r.45.32. In the case of J3, the court will order (as provided by r.36.21(1)(a) and (2)) that the defendant is entitled to the fixed costs in r.45.38 and interest on those costs (r.36.21(4)(c)).

As to the amount of fixed costs (which may vary depending upon whether the court determined the claim on the papers or at a hearing), see rr.45.32 and 45.38.

Where the claimant is entitled to recover from the defendant interest on fixed costs, r.36.21(4)(c) fixes no start date for the running of interest, but limits the rate to a figure not exceeding 10 per cent above base rate. Where the defendant is entitled to recover from the claimant interest on fixed costs, r.36.21(2)(b) provides that it is interest from the first business day after the date of the RTA Protocol offer, but imposes no interest rate cap. (When it is remembered that r.36.18 states that an RTA Protocol offer is deemed to be made "on the first business day after" the Court Proceedings Pack is sent to the defendant, it seems odd that the phrase "from the first business day after" should have been included in r.36.21(2)(b).)

Deduction of benefits

36.22 **36.22 For the purposes of rule 36.21(1)(a) the amount of the judgment is less than the RTA Protocol offer where the judgment is less than that offer once deductible amounts identified in the judgment are deducted.**

("Deductible amount" is defined in rule 36.15(1)(d).)

Effect of rule

For effect of r.36.21(1)(a), see para.36.21.1 above. **36.22.1**

PART 44

GENERAL RULES ABOUT COSTS

Costs–only proceedings

In rule 44.12A(4A) for "Section II of Part 45" substitute:

Section II or Section VI of Part 45 **44.12A**

Comment

At the end of the first paragraph add:

Sections II and VI of Pt 45 (referred to in r.44.12A(4A), as amended by the Civil Procedure (Amendment) Rules 2010, impose fixed recoverable costs regimes on, respectively, certain proceedings arising from road traffic accidents, and on claims that have been started (or should have been started) under Practice Direction 8B (Pre–Action Protocol for Low Value Personal Injury Claims in Road Traffic Accidents—Stage 3 Procedure). Practice Direction 8B sets out the procedure for a claim where the parties have followed the Pre–Action Protocol for Low Value Personal Injury Claims in Road Traffic Accidents ("the RTA Protocol"). There are two sequential stages to the Protocol process, Stage 1 and Stage 2, which the parties are expected to follow, before embarking (if necessary) on court proceedings in accordance with the procedures set out in Practice Direction 8B ("the Stage 3 procedure") (see further, as to the RTA Protocol processes Stage 1 and Stage 2, para.C13A–001 below, and as to the Stage 3 Procedure, para.8BPD.0 above). During the Stage 1 and 2 processes, upon the happening of certain events in negotiations for settlement, the claimant may become entitled to fixed costs (as provided by Sect.VI of Pt 45) and to certain disbursements. Where there is a dispute as to the amount or validity of any disbursement, the parties may use the procedure set out in r.44.12A (RTA Protocol para.7.38). **44.12A.1**

Costs–only application after a claim is started under Part 8 in accordance with Practice Direction 8B

Add new rule 44.12C:

44.12C—(1) This rule sets out the procedure where— **44.12C**

(a) the parties to adispute have reached an agreement on all issues (including which party is to pay the costs) which is made or confirmed in writing; but

(b) they have failed to agree the amount of those costs; and

(c) proceedings have been started under Part 8 in accordance with Practice Direction 8B.

(2) Either party may make an application for the court to determine the costs.

(3) Where an application is made under this rule the court will assess the costs in accordance with rule 45.34 or rule 45.37.

(4) Rule 48.3 (amount of costs where costs are payable pursuant to a contract) does not apply to an application under this rule.

(Practice Direction 8B sets out the procedure for a claim where the parties have followed the Pre–Action Protocol for Low Value Personal Injury Claims in Road Traffic Accidents.)

Effect of rule

44.12C.1 The procedure set out in this rule describes a procedure for making an application in the course of proceedings; see further commentary following r.45.36.

PART 45

FIXED COSTS

Editorial introduction

Add new paragraph at end:

45.0.2 Section VI imposes a fixed recoverable costs regime on claims that have been started (or should have been started) under Practice Direction 8B (Pre-Action Protocol for Low Value Personal Injury Claims in Road Traffic Accidents—Stage 3 Procedure). See further commentary following r.45.27 below.

II. Road Traffic Accidents—Fixed Recoverable Costs

Scope and interpretation

Delete rule 45.7(3) and substitute:

45.7 **45.7—(3) This Section does not apply where—**

(a) the claimant is a litigant in person; or

(b) Section VI of this Part applies.

III. Fixed Percentage Increase in Road Traffic Accident Claims

Scope and interpretation

Add new rule 45.15(4)(d):

45.15 **(d) to a claim to which Section VI of this Part applies.**

Note

Add new paragraph at end:

45.15.1 Section VI of this Part (referred to in r.45.15(4)) imposes a fixed recoverable costs regime on claims that have been started (or should have been started) under Practice Direction 8B (Pre-Action Protocol for Low Value Personal Injury Claims in Road Traffic Accidents—Stage 3 Procedure).

VI. Pre-Action Protocol for Low Value Personal Injury Claims in Road Traffic Accidents

Scope and interpretation

Add new paragraphs 45.27 to 45.40.1:

45.27 **45.27—(1) This Section applies to claims that have been or should have been started under Part 8 in accordance with Practice Direction 8B ("the Stage 3 Procedure").**

(2) Where a party has not complied with the RTA Protocol rule 45.36 will apply.

(3) "RTA Protocol" means the Pre-Action Protocol for Personal Injury Claims in Road Traffic Accidents.

(4) A reference to "Claim Notification Form" is a reference to the form used in the RTA Protocol.

The Stage 3 procedure and fixed costs

Practice Direction 8B sets out the procedure, referred to in the Pre-Action Protocol for Low Value Personal Injury Claims in Road Traffic Accidents ("the RTA Protocol") as "the Stage 3 Procedure", for a claim in which the parties have followed the Stage 1 process and (liability having been admitted) the Stage 2 process as set out in the RTA Protocol but were unable, at the end of Stage 2, to agree the amount of damages payable. The claim is made pursuant to Pt 8 as modified by PD 8B. The Stage 3 Procedure also applies where the parties were able to reach agreement at the end of Stage 2 but, because the claimant was a child, the approval of the court is required in relation to the settlement in accordance with r.21.10(2) (see further rr.45.33 to 45.35). **45.27.1**

The provisions of the fixed costs regime set out in Section VI of Pt 45 are in many respects similar to those found in the fixed costs regimes contained in other Sections of Pt 45. However, its effects extend beyond the award of costs in court proceedings as claimants may become entitled to costs during the Stage 1 and Stage 2 pre-action processes, and not merely after court proceedings have been started under the Stage 3 procedure (see further para.45.29.1 below). Section III (Fixed Percentage Increase in Road Traffic Accident Claims) of Pt 45 does not apply to a claim to which Section VI of the Part applies.

Application of fixed costs, disbursements and success fee

45.28 The only costs allowed are— **45.28**

(a) fixed costs in rule 45.29;

(b) disbursements in accordance with rule 45.30; and

(c) a success fee in accordance with rule 45.31.

Amount of fixed costs

45.29—(1) Subject to paragraph (4), the amount of fixed costs is set out in Table 1. **45.29**

(2) In Table 1—

(a) "Type A fixed costs" means the legal representative's costs;

(b) "Type B fixed costs" means the advocate's costs; and

(c) "Type C fixed costs" means the costs for the advice on the amount of damages where the claimant is a child.

(3) "Advocate" has the same meaning as in rule 46.1(2)(a).

(4) Subject to rule 45.36(2), the court will not award more or less than the amounts shown in Table 1.

(5) Where the claimant—

(a) lives or works in an area set out in the Costs Practice Direction; and

(b) instructs a legal representative who practises in that area,

the fixed costs will include, in addition to the costs set out in Table 1, an amount equal to 12.5% of the Stage 1 and 2 and Stage 3 Type A fixed costs.

(6) Where appropriate, value added tax (VAT) may be recovered in addition to the amount of fixed costs and any reference in this Section to fixed costs is a reference to those costs net of any such VAT.

Table 1—fixed costs in relation to the RTA Protocol	
Stage 1 fixed costs—	**£400**
Stage 2 fixed Costs—	**£800**

Stage 3—		
	Type A fixed costs—	£250
	Type B fixed costs—	£250
	Type C fixed costs—	£150

Fixed costs—when payable

45.29.1 Rule 45.27 states that this Section applies to claims that have been or should have been started under Practice Direction 8B. Where court proceedings are started under Pt 8 in accordance with Practice Direction 8B ("the Stage 3 Procedure") the claimant must file the claim form and must file with it certain documents (para.6.1). Complying with that requirement represents the start of the Stage 3 Procedure for the purposes of fixed costs (para.6.2). The fixed costs in r.45.29 apply in relation to a claimant only where a claimant has a legal representative (RTA Protocol para.4.5). Where, in proceedings to which Section VI applies, a child is a party (whether claimant or defendant) the court will not make an order for detailed assessment of the costs payable to the child, but will assess the costs in the manner set out in Section VI (r.21.10(3) (see further r.45.33 to 45.35).

Paragraph 7.67 of the RTA Protocol states that, where the claimant gives notice to the defendant that the claim is unsuitable for this Protocol, then the claim will no longer continue under this Protocol. However, where the court considers that the claimant acted unreasonably in giving such notice it will award no more than the fixed costs in r.45.29.

The fixed costs regime set out in Section VI of Pt 45 applies during the pre–action processes set out in the RTA Protocol and with which parties are expected to comply before starting proceedings. Paragraph 7.53 of the Protocol states that, where the parties agree to settle during Stage 2 of the Protocol process, on terms that the defendant within a particular time should pay the claimant damages, the defendant should pay to the claimant those damages, together with any unpaid Stage 1 fixed costs in r.45.29, the Stage 2 fixed costs in that rule, and relevant disbursements allowed in accordance with r.45.30. (Any offer to settle made at any stage by either party must include the Stage 2 fixed costs in r.45.29 (ibid para.7.37).)

Paragraph 7.61 of the RTA Protocol states that, where the parties are unable to agree the amount of damages payable at the end of the Stage 2 process of the Protocol, the defendants must pay to the claimant their final offer of damages, again together with any unpaid Stage 1 fixed costs in r.45.29, the Stage 2 fixed costs in that rule, and, if they have not been agreed, disbursements in accordance with r.45.30(2) which the defendant believes to be reasonable ("a non–settlement payment"). (Where disbursements are disputed, the parties may have recourse to the procedure in r.44.12A (Costs–only proceedings).)

Other provisions in the RTA Protocol which have the effect of requiring fixed costs to be paid by one party to another before court proceedings are started without recourse to the court for a costs order being required (unless the paying party fails to comply) are: para.5.9 (Claimant's reasonable belief of the value of the claim), and para.6.18 (liability admitted under Stage 1).

Where, in proceedings under the Stage 3 Procedure, the court considers that further evidence must be provided by any party, and the claim is not suitable to continue under that procedure, and orders that the claim will continue under Pt 7, the court will not allow the Stage 3 fixed costs (Practice Direction 8B para.7.2).

Disbursements

45.30 **45.30—(1) The court—**

(a) may allow a claim for a disbursement of a type mentioned in paragraph (2); but

(b) must not allow a claim for any other type of disbursement.

(2) The disbursements referred to in paragraph (1) are—

(a) the cost of obtaining—

(i) medical records;

(ii) a medical report or reports as provided for in the RTA Protocol;

(iii) an engineer's report;

(iv) a search of the records of the—

(aa) Driver Vehicle Licensing Authority;

(bb) Motor Insurance Database;

(b) the amount of the insurance premium or, where a membership organisation undertakes to meet liabilities incurred to pay the costs of other parties to proceedings, a sum not exceeding such additional amount of costs as would be allowed under section 30 of the Access to Justice Act 1999 in respect of provision made against the risk of having to meet such liabilities;

(c) court fees as a result of Part 21 being applicable;

(d) court fees payable where proceedings are started as a result of a limitation period that is about to expire;

(e) court fees in respect of the Stage 3 procedure;

(f) any other disbursement that has arisen due to a particular feature of the dispute.

(Insurance premium is defined in rule 43.2(1)(m).)

(Membership organisation is defined in rule 43.2(1)(n).)

Effect of rule

Where the parties agree to settle during Stage 2 of the RTA Protocol process, on terms that the defendant should pay the claimant damages, the defendant must pay the disbursements in r.45.30(2)(a) within a particular time as provided by para.7.53 of the RTA Protocol. (Any offer to settle made at any stage by either party must include an agreement in principle to pay disbursements (ibid para.7.37).) **45.30.1**

Paragraph 7.24 of the RTA Protocol states that, in court proceedings under the Stage 3 procedure set out in PD 8B, the court may refuse to allow, the costs of a further initial medical report obtained by the claimant without recommendation from a medical expert.

Success fee

45.31—(1) A party who has entered into a funding arrangement of a type specified in rule 43.2(1)(k)(i) in respect of any element of the fixed costs in rule 45.29 may recover a success fee on that element of the fixed costs. **45.31**

(2) A reference to a success fee in this Section is a reference to a success fee in accordance with paragraph (1).

(3) Where the court—

(a) determines the claim at a Stage 3 hearing or on the papers; and

(b) awards an amount of damages that is more than the defendant's RTA Protocol offer,

the amount of the claimant's success fee is—

(i) 12.5% of the Stage 1 and 2 fixed costs; and

(ii) 100% of the relevant Stage 3 fixed costs.

(RTA Protocol offer is defined in rule 36.17.)

(4) Where the court—

(a) determines the claim at a Stage 3 hearing or on the papers; and
(b) awards an amount of damages that is equal to or less than the defendant's RTA Protocol offer,

the amount of the defendant's success fee is 100% of the relevant Stage 3 fixed costs.

(5) Where the claimant is a child and the court—
(a) does not approve a settlement at a settlement hearing;
(b) determines the claim at a Stage 3 hearing; and
(c) awards an amount of damages that is more than the amount of the settlement considered by the court at the first settlement hearing;

the amount of the claimant's success fee is—
(i) 12.5% of the Stage 1 and 2 fixed costs; and
(ii) 100% of the relevant Stage 3 fixed costs.

(6) Where paragraphs (3) to (5) do not apply the success fee is—
(a) 12.5% of Stage 1 and 2 fixed costs; and
(b) 12.5% of the relevant Stage 3 fixed costs.

(7) The amount of the success fee set out in paragraphs (3) to (6) will be calculated without regard to any additional amount which may be included in the fixed costs by virtue of rule 45.29(5).

Effect of rule

45.31.1 Where the parties agree to settle during Stage 2 of the RTA Protocol processes, on terms that the defendant should pay the claimant damages, the defendant must pay a success fee in accordance with r.43.2(1)(k)(i) for Stage 1 and Stage 2 fixed costs within a particular time as provided by para.7.44 of the RTA Protocol. (Any offer to settle made at any stage by either party must include a success fee in accordance with r.45.31(1) (RTA Protocol para.7.37).)

As to meanings of "settlement hearing" and of "Stage 3 hearing", see Practice Direction 8B paras 3.3 and 3.4, and commentary following r.45.34 below.

In the text of para.(5) of this rule as enacted, the word "and" was omitted at the end of sub–para.(c)(i), although it was included in drafts of the rule. That omission would appear to be inadvertent and has been rectified in the text as printed above.

Where the claimant obtains judgment for an amount more than the defendant's RTA Protocol offer

45.32 **45.32 Where rule 36.21(1)(b) or (c) applies, the court will order the defendant to pay—**

(a) where not already paid by the defendant, the Stage 1 and 2 fixed costs;

(b) where the claim is determined—
(i) on the papers, Stage 3 Type A fixed costs;
(ii) at a Stage 3 hearing, Stage 3 Type A and B fixed costs; or
(iii) at a Stage 3 hearing and the claimant is a child, Type A, B and C fixed costs;

(c) disbursements allowed in accordance with rule 45.30; and

(d) a success in accordance with rule 45.31(3).

Effect of rule

45.32.1 See further commentary following r.36.21. As to meaning of "Stage 3 hearing", see Practice Direction 8B para.3.4, and commentary following r.45.34 below.

Settlement at Stage 2 where the claimant is a child

45.33 **45.33—(1) This rule applies where—**

(a) the claimant is a child;
(b) there is a settlement at Stage 2 of the RTA Protocol; and
(c) an application is made to the court to approve of the settlement.

(2) Where the court approves the settlement at a settlement hearing it will order the defendant to pay—
(a) the Stage 1 and 2 fixed costs;
(b) the Stage 3 Type A, B and C fixed costs;
(c) disbursements allowed in accordance with rule 45.30; and
(d) a success fee in accordance with rule 45.31(6).

(3) Where the court does not approve the settlement at a settlement hearing it will order the defendant to pay the Stage 1 and 2 fixed costs.

(4) Paragraphs (5) and (6) apply where the court does not approve the settlement at the first settlement hearing but does approve the settlement at a second settlement hearing.

(5) At the second settlement hearing the court will order the defendant to pay—
(a) the Stage 3 Type A and C fixed costs for the first settlement hearing;
(b) disbursements allowed in accordance with rule 45.30;
(c) the Stage 3 Type B fixed costs for one of the hearings; and
(d) a success fee in accordance with rule 45.31(6) on the Stage 1 and 2 fixed costs and the Stage 3 Type A, B and C fixed costs.

(6) The court in its discretion may also order—
(a) the defendant to pay—
(i) an additional amount of either or both the Stage 3—
(aa) Type A fixed costs;
(bb) Type B fixed costs; and
(ii) a success fee in accordance with rule 45.31(6) on the additional Stage 3 fixed costs in sub–paragraph (a)(i); or
(b) the claimant to pay an amount equivalent to either or both the Stage 3—
(i) Type A fixed costs;
(ii) Type B fixed costs.

Note

As to the payment of costs in accordance with r.45.33 were there has been a settlement at Stage 2 of the RTA Protocol processes and the claimant is a child, see further Practice Direction 8B paras 12.1 to 12.3. As to meaning of a "settlement hearing", see Practice Direction 8B para.3.3, and commentary following r.45.34 below. **45.33.1**

Settlement at Stage 3 where the claimant is a child

45.34—(1) This rule applies where— **45.34**
(a) the claimant is a child;
(b) there is a settlement after proceedings are started under the Stage 3 Procedure;
(c) the settlement is more than the defendant's RTA Protocol offer; and

(d) an application is made to the court to approve the settlement.

(2) Where the court approves the settlement at the settlement hearing it will order the defendant to pay—

(a) the Stage 1 and 2 fixed costs;

(b) the Stage 3 Type A, B and C fixed costs;

(c) disbursements allowed in accordance with rule 45.30; and

(d) a success fee in accordance with rule 45.31(6).

(3) Where the court does not approve the settlement at the settlement hearing it will order the defendant to pay the Stage 1 and 2 fixed costs.

(4) Paragraphs (5) and (6) apply where the court does not approve the settlement at the first settlement hearing but does approve the settlement at the Stage 3 hearing.

(5) At the Stage 3 hearing the court will order the defendant to pay—

(a) the Stage 3 Type A and C fixed costs for the settlement hearing;

(b) disbursements allowed in accordance with rule 45.30;

(c) the Stage 3 Type B fixed costs for one of the hearings; and

(d) a success fee in accordance with rule 45.31(6) on the Stage 1 and 2 fixed costs and the Stage 3 Type A, B and C fixed costs.

(6) The court in its discretion may also order—

(a) the defendant to pay—

(i) an additional amount of either or both of the Stage 3—

(aa) Type A fixed costs;

(bb) Type B fixed costs; and

(ii) a success fee in accordance with rule 45.31(6) on the additional Stage 3 fixed costs in sub–paragraph (a)(i); or

(b) the claimant to pay an amount equivalent to either or both of the Stage 3—

(i) Type A fixed costs;

(ii) Type B fixed costs.

(7) Where the settlement is not approved at the Stage 3 hearing the court will order the defendant to pay the Stage 3 Type A fixed costs.

Effect of rule

45.34.1 As to the payment of costs in accordance with r.45.34 were there has been a settlement in proceedings under the Stage 3 Procedure and the claimant is a child, see further Practice Direction 8B paras 13.1 to 13.3.

A "settlement hearing" is a hearing where the court considers a settlement agreed between the parties, whether before court proceedings have been started in relation to a claim to which the RTA Protocol applies, or after, and the claimant is child (Practice Direction 8B para.3.3).

A "Stage 3 hearing" means a final hearing under the Stage 3 Procedure as set out in Practice Direction 8B to determine the amount of damages in a claim to which the RTA Protocol applies, or after, and the claimant is child (Practice Direction 8B para.3.4).

Where the court orders the claim is not suitable to be determined under the Stage 3 procedure and the claimant is a child

45.35 **Where—** 45.35

(a) the claimant is a child; and

(b) at a settlement hearing or the Stage 3 hearing the court orders that the claim is not suitable to be determined under the Stage 3 procedure,

the court will order the defendant to pay—

(i) the Stage 1 and 2 fixed costs; and

(ii) the Stage 3 Type A, B and C fixed costs.

Effect of rule

Paragraph 12.5 of Practice Direction 8B states that, where the settlement is not approved at the first settlement hearing and the court orders that the claim is not suitable to be determined under the Stage 3 Procedure, the court will order costs to be paid in accordance with r.45.35 and will give directions. 45.35.1

As to meanings of "settlement hearing" and of "Stage 3 hearing", see Practice Direction 8B paras 3.3 and 3.4, and commentary following r.45.34 above.

Failure to comply or electing not to continue with the RTA Protocol—costs consequences

45.36—(1) This rule applies where the claimant— 45.36

(a) does not comply with the process set out in the RTA Protocol; or

(b) elects not to continue with that process,

and starts proceedings under Part 7.

(2) Where a judgment is given in favour of the claimant but—

(a) the court determines that the defendant did not proceed with the process set out in the RTA Protocol because the claimant provided insufficient information on the Claim Notification Form;

(b) the court considers that the claimant acted unreasonably—

(i) by discontinuing the process set out in the RTA Protocol and starting proceedings under Part 7;

(ii) by valuing the claim at more than £10,000, so that the claimant did not need to comply with the RTA Protocol; or

(iii) except for paragraph (2)(a), in any other way that caused the process in the RTA Protocol to be discontinued; or

(c) the claimant did not comply with the RTA Protocol at all despite the claim falling within the scope of the RTA Protocol;

the court may order the defendant to pay no more than the fixed costs in rule 45.29 together with the disbursements allowed in accordance with rule 45.30 and success fee in accordance with rule 45.31(3).

(3) Where the claimant starts proceedings under paragraph 7.22 of the RTA Protocol and the court orders the defendant to make an interim payment of no more than the interim payment made under paragraph 7.14(2) or (3) of that Protocol the court will, on the final determination of the proceedings, order the defendant to pay no more than—

(a) the Stage 1 and 2 fixed costs;
(b) the disbursements allowed in accordance with rule 45.30; and
(c) a success fee in accordance with rule 45.31(3).

Effect of rule

45.36.1 In proceedings under the Stage 3 Procedure, the court may dismiss the claim because the defendant opposed it on the grounds that the claimant had not followed the procedure set out in the RTA Protocol, or had filed and served additional or new evidence with the claim form that had not been provided under the RTA Protocol (Practice Direction 8B para.9.1). In these circumstances the court will not allow the Stage 3 fixed costs and the costs consequences stated in r.45.36 will apply to any proceedings under Pt 7 started by the claimant.

Provisions in the RTA Protocol expressly stating that, in particular circumstances, the claimant may discontinue the Protocol processes and start proceedings under Pt 7 are: paras 7.21, 7.33, 7.39 and 7.58. Other provisions in the RTA Protocol state that, in other circumstances, claims "will no longer continue under this RTA Protocol", thereby implying that, if the claimant wishes to pursue the claim, court proceedings should be started under Pt 7; see e.g. paras 4.2, 6.8, 6.19, 7.22, 7.32 and 7.67 (cf. para.6.15). Paragraph 7.22 states that a claimant dissatisfied with the amount of an interim payment made by a defendant under Stage 2 of the Protocol process may start proceedings under Pt 7 and recites the terms of r.45.36(3) (but not wholly accurately). In the circumstances provided for in para.7.19 (Request for an interim payment where the claimant is a child), a claimant may start proceedings under Pt 7 without whilst continuing to comply with the RTA Protocols processes and running no risk of being exposed to the costs penalties in r.35.36.

Rule 45.40 applies where the court makes an order for costs in circumstances where the claim no longer continues under the RTA Protocol.

Where the parties have settled after proceedings have started

45.37 **45.37—(1) This rule applies where an application is made under rule 44.12C (costs–only application after a claim is started under Part 8 in accordance with Practice Direction 8B).**

(2) Where the settlement is more than the defendant's RTA Protocol offer the court will order the defendant to pay—
(a) the Stage 1 and 2 fixed costs where not already paid by the defendant;
(b) the Stage 3 Type A fixed costs;
(c) disbursements allowed in accordance with rule 45.30; and
(d) a success fee in accordance with rule 45.31(6).

(3) Where the settlement is less than or equal to the defendant's RTA Protocol offer the court will order the defendant to pay—
(a) the Stage 1 and 2 fixed costs where not already paid by the defendant;
(b) disbursements allowed in accordance with rule 45.30; and
(c) a success fee in accordance with rule 45.31(6).

(4) The court may, in its discretion, order either party to pay the costs of the application.

Effect of rule

45.37.1 Where proceedings have been started under Practice Direction 8B, and the parties have reached an agreement on all issues but have failed to agree the amount of costs, either party may make an application for the court to determine the costs (r.44.12C).

Where no proceedings have been started (whether under Practice Direction 8B or otherwise), and the parties have reached an agreement on all issues but have failed to agree the amount of costs, either party may start costs–only proceedings under r.44.12A. Paragraph (4A) of r.44.12A states that, in those circumstances, if the proceedings in which the parties failed to reach an agreement as to the amount of costs were "proceedings to which Section VI of Part 45 applies", the court shall asses the costs in the manner set out in that Section. In this context, "proceedings to which Section VI of Part 45 applies" must mean claims that should have been started under Practice Direction 8B (see r.45.27(1)).

Where the claimant obtains judgment for an amount equal to or less than the defendant's RTA Protocol offer

45.38 Where rule 36.21(1)(a) applies, the court will order the claimant to pay— 45.38

(a) where the claim is determined—

(i) on the papers, Stage 3 Type A fixed costs; or

(ii) at a hearing, Stage 3 Type A and B fixed costs;

(b) disbursements allowed in accordance with rule 45.30; and

(c) a success fee in accordance with rule 45.31(4).

Interest on costs

The defendant is entitled to interest on these fixed costs as provided by r.36.21(2)(b). 45.38.1

Adjournment

45.39 Where the court adjourns a settlement hearing or a Stage 3 hearing it may, in its discretion, order a party to pay— 45.39

(a) an additional amount of the Stage 3 Type B fixed costs; and

(b) any court fee for that adjournment.

Costs on adjournment of hearings

As to meanings of "settlement hearing" and of "Stage 3 hearing", see Practice Direction 8B paras 3.3 and 3.4, and commentary following r.45.34 above. 45.39.1

Account of payment of Stage 1 fixed costs

45.40 Where a claim no longer continues under the RTA Protocol the court will, when making any order as to costs including an order for fixed recoverable costs under Section II of this Part, take into account the Stage 1 fixed costs together with any success fee on those costs that have been paid by the defendant. 45.40

Effect of rule

It would seem that, in this rule, "claim" means a claim that has been, or should have been started under Pt 8 in accordance with Practice Direction 8B (see r.45.27(1)), and therefore the rule speaks to the circumstance in which the court makes an order for costs when a claim no longer continues under that procedure. However, it may be that it is intended that the rule should also take effect in those circumstances where the court makes an order for costs upon a claim no longer continuing under the Stage 2 process of the RTA Protocol and fixed costs become payable (pursuant to a court order if necessary); see further para.45.29.1. 45.40.1

THE COSTS PRACTICE DIRECTION (CPR PT 45)

Fixed Costs

Additional costs for work in specified areas

In paragraph 25A.6, delete "rule 45.9(2)" and substitute:

rules 45.9(2) and 45.29(5) 45PD.6

PART 46

FAST TRACK TRIAL COSTS

Comment

In the second paragraph, for "£350" substitute:

46.3.1 £485

PART 48

COSTS—SPECIAL CASES

Costs where money is payable by or to a child or protected party

In rule 48.5(2)(ii) for "Section II of Part 45 applies" substitute:

48.5 **Section II or Section VI of Part 45 applies**

Editorial note

Add new paragraph at end:

48.5.1 Sections II and VI of Part 45 (referred to in r.48.5(2)(b)) impose fixed recoverable costs regimes on, respectively, certain proceedings arising from road traffic accidents, and on claims that have been started (or should have been started) under Practice Direction 8B (Pre-Action Protocol for Low Value Personal Injury Claims in Road Traffic Accidents—Stage 3 Procedure).

PART 52

APPEALS

PRACTICE DIRECTION 52—APPEALS

Documents

52PD.19 *Add at start of paragraph 5.6A(1)(f):*

except where sub-paragraph (1A) applies

Add new paragraph 5.6A(1A):

(1A) Where the appeal relates to a judgment following a determination on the papers under Part 8 in accordance with Practice Direction 8B, the appellant must include in the appeal bundle the order made by the court containing the reasons for the award of damages. A transcript of the judgment is not required.

PART 55

POSSESSION CLAIMS

I. General Rules

Possession claims relating to mortgaged residential property

Add new paragraph (2)(c):

(c) any registered proprietor (other than the claimant) of a registered charge over the property. **55.10**

II. Accelerated Possession Claims of Property Let on an Assured Shorthold Tenancy

When this section may be used

At the end of rule 55.11(3) (after "a registered social landlord") add:

or a private registered provider of social housing **55.11**

PART 65

PROCEEDINGS RELATING TO ANTI-SOCIAL BEHAVIOUR AND HARASSMENT

I. Housing Act 1996 Injunctions

Issuing the Claim

In paragraph 1.1, for "Practice Direction 8" substitute:

Practice Direction 8B **65PD.1**

III. Demotion or Suspension Claims

Demotion Claims Made in the Alternative to Possession Claims

In paragraph 5.1(2) for "or a registered social landlord" substitute:

, a registered social landlord or a private registered provider of social housing **65PD.5**

Particulars of Claim

In paragraph 7.1(2) for "or a registered social landlord" substitute:

, a registered social landlord or a private registered provider of social housing **65PD.7**

VII. Parenting Orders under the Anti-Social Behaviour Act 2003

Applications for Parenting Orders

In paragraph 16.1, add after "a registered social landlord":

or a private registered provider of social housing **65PD.16**

SECTION C

PRE–ACTION PROTOCOLS

PRACTICE DIRECTION—PRE-ACTION CONDUCT

ANNEX A—Guidance on pre–action procedure where no pre–action protocol or other formal pre–action procedure applies

3. Defendant's acknowledgment of the letter before claim

In sub–paragraph 3.4, for "has not complied" substitute:

C1–009 has complied

The Letter of Claim

Add new paragraph 2.10A:

C2–005 **2.10A** Where a claim no longer continues under the Pre–Action Protocol for Low Value Personal Injury Claims in Road Traffic Accidents the Claim Notification Form ("CNF") completed by the claimant under that Protocol can be used as the letter of claim under this Protocol unless the defendant has notified the claimant that there is inadequate information in the CNF.

3.

The Protocol

Letter of Claim

In paragraph 3.1, for "The claimant" substitute:

C2–012 Subject to paragraph 2.10A the claimant

PRE–ACTION PROTOCOL FOR POSSESSION CLAIMS BASED ON RENT ARREARS

Aims and scope of the protocol

In the first paragraph, add after "Housing Action Trusts":

C11–001 and private registered providers of social housing

In the second paragraph, add after "given to social landlords":

and private registered providers

In the last paragraph, add after "Registered Social Landlords":

, private registered providers of social housing

PRE–ACTION PROTOCOL FOR LOW VALUE PERSONAL INJURY CLAIMS IN ROAD TRAFFIC ACCIDENTS

Editorial introduction

Add new paragraphs C13A–001 to C13A–006:

C13A–001 Practice Direction (Pre–Action Conduct) (see para.C1–001 above) contains provisions describing "the conduct the court will normally expect of the prospective parties prior to the start of proceedings". The court will expect the parties to have complied with that practice direction "or any relevant pre–action protocol". The table following para.5.2 lists the pre–action protocols currently in force (see para.C1–005 above).

In March 2010, by CPR TSO Update 52, a further pre–action protocol, the Pre–Action Protocol for Low Value Personal Injury Claims in Road Traffic Accidents ("the RTA Protocol") was published. It applies where (1) a claim for damages arises from a road traffic accident occurring on or after April 30, 2010; (2) the claim includes damages in respect of personal injury; (3) the claimant values the claim at not more than £10,000 on a full liability basis including pecuniary losses but excluding interest; and (4) if proceedings were started the small claims track would not be the normal track for that claim (para.4.1). The aim of the RTA Protocol is to ensure that (1) the defendant pays damages and costs using the process set out in the Protocol without the need for the claimant to start proceedings; (2) the payment of damages is made within a reasonable time; and (3) the claimant's legal representative receives the fixed costs at the end of each stage in this Protocol (para.3.1).

The RTA Protocol describes in great detail the behaviour the court will normally expect of parties, of their legal representatives and of their insurers, involved in claims of the type to which it applies. The Protocol accepts that, and is structured on the basis that, in personal injury road accident cases, insurers are the real party at interest on the defence side. A striking feature is that, insofar as the Protocol requires parties, lawyers and insurers to send information one to another, it is expected that it will be sent electronically (para.5.2). To facilitate this insurers writing road accident insurance have cooperated in creating an electronic address through which they should be contacted by other parties engaged in RTA Protocol claims (see para.5.1 of the Protocol).

Where a claimant does not comply with the RTA Protocol, or elects not to continue with the processes therein, and starts court proceedings under CPR Pt 7 and obtains judgment, the court may order the defendant to pay no more than the fixed costs in r.45.29, together with the disbursements set out in r.45.30 and success fee in accordance with r.45.31(3) (see r.45.36). Generally, the sanction in the hands of a claimant faced with a defendant who does not cooperate in working through the RTA Protocol processes properly is that of starting court proceedings in the normal way (under Pt 7), thereby exposing the defendant (in the event of the claimant obtaining judgment) to much greater costs than those that would be payable under the fixed costs regime applicable when cases are disposed of under the Protocol processes, or under the bespoke court procedures to which the Protocol processes lead (see explanation of "the Stage 3 Procedure" below).

Summary of Stage 1 and Stage 2 processes

In the RTA Protocol a "claim" means "a claim, prior to the start of proceedings, for payment of damages" under the Protocol process (para.1.1(1)). There are two sequential stages to the Protocol processes, Stage 1 and Stage 2, which may be followed by "the Stage 3 procedure" (see further below). **C13A–002**

The principal objective of Stage 1 (paras 6.1 to 6.18) is to provide a process under which the defendant's insurers can admit liability promptly (generally within 15 days) enabling the parties to concentrate on the issue of quantum by following the Stage 2 process (para.6.11). Stage 1 begins when a claimant (i.e. "a person starting a claim under this Protocol" para.1.1(2)) completes and sends to the insurer of the defendant (i.e. "the person who is subject to the claim") a Claim Notification Form (Form RTA 1) (CNF), and at the same time sends to the defendant the Defendant Only Claim Notification Form (Form RTA 2). Within 15 days the defendant must complete and send to the claimant the "Insurer Response" section of the CNF. Amongst other things, that section invites the defendant to state whether liability is admitted or not. Where liability is admitted the defendant must within 10 days pay the claimant the Stage 1 fixed costs (para.6.18). The claim does not continue to Stage 2 where the defendant does not admit liability or makes an admission of liability but alleges contributory negligence (other than in relation to the claimant's admitted failure to wear a seat belt) (para.6.15). Where for these reasons the claim does not continue to Stage 2 the claim proceeds under the Pre–Action Protocol for Personal Injury Claims (see C2–001 above), starting at para.3.7 of that Protocol (which allows a maximum of three months for the defendant to investigate the claim) (para.6.17).

Stage 2 of the RTA Protocol process (paras 7.1 to 7.67) proceeds on the assumption that the objective is to enable the parties to settle issues of quantum by negotiation. It is a highly prescriptive process. There are detailed provisions about the providing of medical reports and, where the Protocol process is stayed (para.7.7), about the making of interim payments by the defendant on account of damages claimed by the claimant (paras 7.8 to 7.16). Under the Stage 2 process as it develops the claimant is required to send to the defendant the Interim Settlement Pack Form (Form RTA 4) and the Stage 2 Settlement Pack Form (Form RTA 5).

In certain circumstances, the claim will no longer continue under this Protocol. The most obvious one is that of the defendant not admitting liability under Stage 1 process (para.6.15). Events occurring under Stage 2 that may or must result in the claim no longer continuing under the Protocol include, for example, those described in paras 7.21 to 7.23 (defendant failing to make interim payments), and para.7.32 (within initial consideration period, defendant withdrawing an admission of causation). The Protocol "ceases to apply" to a claim where, at any stage, the claimant notifies the defendant that the claim has now been revalued at a value taking it beyond the £10,000 limit (para.4.2).

Where the parties, having followed the Stage 1 and Stage 2 processes and do not reach agreement, the claimant must send the Court Proceedings Pack (Part A and Part B) Form (Forms RTA 6 and RTA 7) to the defendant.

In certain circumstances, fixed costs are recoverable by the claimant under the Stage 1 and Stage 2 processes and must be paid by the defendant.

The Stage 3 procedure

C13A-003 Where parties have followed the RTA Protocol and where they are unable to agree the amount of damages payable at the end of the Stage 2 process, a claim may be made using the court procedure ("the Stage 3 procedure") set out under CPR Pt 8 (Alternative Procedure for Claims) in accordance with Practice Direction 8B (Pre-Action Protocol for Low Value Personal Injury Claims in Road Traffic Accidents—Stage 3 Procedure).

A claim is also made under the Stage 3 procedure where the claimant is a child and a settlement has been agreed by the parties at the end of Stage 2, and the approval of the court is required in relation to the settlement in accordance with CPR r.21.10(2).

A claim under Practice Direction 8B must be started in a county court, and will normally be heard by a district judge.

In court proceedings started under the Stage 3 procedure the rules in Sect.II of CPR Pt 36 (Offers to Settle) apply. Rule 36.21 states the costs consequences of an offer to settle set out in the Court Proceedings Pack Form (Part B) ("an "RTA Protocol offer"). An admission made by a party during the RTA Protocol processes is a pre-action admission for the purposes of CPR Pt 14 (Admissions). Rule 14.1B deals with the circumstances in which such an admission may be withdrawn.

Court proceedings started under the Stage 3 Procedure are subject to the fixed costs regime contained in Sect.VI of Pt 45 (Fixed Costs).

For further information on the Stage 3 Procedure, see commentary on Practice Direction 8B, on r.14.1B (Admissions made under the RTA Protocol), on Sect.II of CPR Pt 36 (Offers to Settle), and on Sect.VI of Pt 45 (Fixed Costs).

Limitation period and RTA Protocol processes

C13A-004 Where compliance with the RTA Protocol is not possible before the expiry of the limitation period the claimant may start proceedings and apply to the court for an order to stay those proceedings while the parties take steps to follow this Protocol (para.5.7). Where proceedings are started for this purpose the claimant should use the procedure set out in Pt 8 in accordance with para.16 of Practice Direction 8B. (Court fees payable where proceedings are started as a result of a limitation period that is about to expire is a recoverable disbursement under r.45.30(2).)

Where a claimant started proceedings under para.16 of Practice Direction 8B and obtained an order staying those proceedings the claimant must, in order to invoke the Stage 3 procedure, apply to lift the stay and request directions in those proceedings (para.5.8).

See further, detailed commentary on para.16 of PD 8B (para.8BPD.16.1 above).

Rules, practice direction and pre-action protocol

C13A-005 By definition, the processes set out in the several pre-action protocols that have come into being since the CPR came into effect, are not pre-trial procedures; but they imitate them to an extent. The RTA Protocol imitates them more thoroughly than other pre–action protocols. Procedures that would normally apply at the pre–trial stages in a case where court proceedings are on foot, and the parties are preparing for a trial on quantum of damages, are found in the RTA Protocol; particularly in the Stage 2 processes relating to obtaining and exchanging of medical reports, to the making of offers to settle, and to the making of interim payments. Further, during the working through of the Protocol processes, liability for costs may be incurred and costs may become payable. The Protocol sets out an intense, time–sensitive process for defendant insurer and claimant solicitor negotiation. (There is not one mention of mediation in the Protocol.) The Protocol Stage 1 and 2 processes may be seen as a form of "civil diversion", that provide parties with a structure for clarifying their disputes and negotiating a settlement similar to that provided by the normal CPR pre–trial procedures.

Normally, CPR rules are supplemented directly by practice directions and indirectly by pre–action protocols. Here these relationships are reversed. The RTA Protocol is the primary source governing party behaviour in the claims to which it applies; Practice Direction 8B builds on the Protocol Stage 2 processes and provides special and limited court procedures for the purpose of determining the claim if settlement is not achieved (and for some other purposes); and Sect.II of CPR Pt 36 (RTA Protocol Offers to Settle) and Sect.VI of Pt 45 (Fixed Costs) provide the legal framework, not only for the Stage 3 procedure but also for the pre–action negotiating processes, in effect supplementing Practice Direction 8B and the RTA Protocol.

The terms of the RTA Protocol have to be read closely with the terms of the provisions in Practice Direction 8B (supplementing Pt 8) (see para.8BPD.0 et seq, above), in Sect.II of CPR Pt 36 (see para.36A.1 et seq, above), and in Sect.VI of Pt 45 (see para.45.27 et seq, above). In the commentaries on those provisions, the linkages with provisions in the RTA Protocol (which is set out immediately below) are noted. These various sources complement (and cannot be divorced from) one another. They constitute an integrated scheme for the disposal of low value personal injury claims arising from road traffic accidents.

Forms

Several forms have been specially designed for use by parties engaged in the RTA **C13A–006**
Protocol processes (the "RTA Forms"). They are listed in para.1.3 of the RTA Protocol and are available on the HMCS website through the address given there. Where court proceedings are commenced under Practice Direction 8B, or under Pt 7, in relation to claims to which the Protocol processes have been applied, the usual forms CPR Pt 4 are used. Where, under para.8.1 of Practice Direction 8B, a defendant files and serves an acknowledgment of service the appropriate form is Form **N210B**, a new form specially struck for this procedural purpose and added to Table 1 in the Pt 4 practice direction.

Add new paragraphs C13–001 to C13–009:

Contents **C13–001**

Section I—Introduction

Section III—The Stages Of The Process

Stage 1

Stage 2

Stage 3

SECTION I—INTRODUCTION

Definitions

1.1 In this Protocol— C13–002

(1) 'claim' means a claim, prior to the start of proceedings, for payment of damages under the process set out in this Protocol;

(2) 'claimant' means a person starting a claim under this Protocol;

(3) 'defendant' means the insurer of the person who is subject to the claim under this Protocol, unless the context indicates that it means—

(a) the person who is subject to the claim;

(b) the defendant's legal representative; or

(c) the Motor Insurers' Bureau ('MIB');

(4) 'legal representative' has the same meaning as in rule 2.3(1) of the Civil Procedure Rules 1998;

(5) 'pecuniary losses' means past and future expenses and losses;

(6) 'vehicle related damages' means damages for—

(a) the pre-accident value of the vehicle;

(b) vehicle repair;

(c) vehicle insurance excess;

(d) vehicle hire;

(7) 'child' means a person under 18;

(8) 'business day' means any day except Saturday, Sunday, a bank holiday, Good Friday or Christmas Day;

(9) 'bank holiday' means a bank holiday under the Banking and Financial Dealings Act 1971;

(10) 'road traffic accident' means an accident resulting in bodily injury to any person caused by, or arising out of, the use of a motor vehicle on a road or other public place in England and Wales unless the injury was caused wholly or in part by a breach by the defendant of one or more of the relevant statutory provisions[1] as defined by section 53 of the Health and Safety at Work etc Act 1974;

(11) 'motor vehicle' means a mechanically propelled vehicle intended for use on roads;

(12) 'road' means any highway and any other road to which the public has access and includes bridges over which a road passes;

(13) 'medical expert' means a person who is—

---

[1] Control of Substances Hazardous to Health Regulations 2002 (S.I. 2002/2677); Lifting Operations and Lifting Equipment Regulations 1998 (S.I. 1998/2307); Management of Health and Safety at Work Regulations 1999 (S.I. 1999/3242); Manual Handling Operations Regulations 1992 (S.I. 1992/2793); Personal Protective Equipment at Work Regulations 1992 (S.I. 1992/2966); Provision and Use of Work Equipment Regulations 1998 (S.I. 1998/2306); Work at Height Regulations 2005 (S.I. 2005/735); Workplace (Health, Safety and Welfare) Regulations 1992 (S.I. 1992/3004).

(a) registered with the General Medical Council;
(b) registered with the General Dental Council; or
(c) a Psychologist or Physiotherapist registered with the Health Professions Council;

(14) 'admission of liability' means the defendant admits that—
(a) the accident occurred;
(b) the accident was caused by the defendant's breach of duty; and
(c) the defendant caused some loss to the claimant, the nature and extent of which is not admitted;

(15) 'deductible amount' has the same meaning as in rule 36.15(1)(d) of the Civil Procedure Rules 1998; and

(16) 'certificate of recoverable benefits' has the same meaning as in rule 36.15(1)(e)(i) of the Civil Procedure Rules 1998.

1.2 A reference to a rule or practice direction, unless otherwise defined, is a reference to a rule in the Civil Procedure Rules 1998 ('CPR') or a practice direction supplementing them.

1.3 Subject to paragraph 1.4 the standard forms used in the process set out in this Protocol are available from Her Majesty's Court Service ('HMCS') website at www.hmcourts–service.gov.uk—
(1) Claim Notification Form ('Form RTA 1');
(2) Defendant Only Claim Notification Form ('Form RTA 2');
(3) Medical Report Form ('Form RTA 3');
(4) Interim Settlement Pack Form ('Form RTA 4');
(5) Stage 2 Settlement Pack Form ('Form RTA 5');
(6) Court Proceedings Pack (Part A) Form ('Form RTA 6'); and
(7) Court Proceedings Pack (Part B) Form ('Form RTA 7').

1.4 The information required in Form RTA 3 may be provided in a different format to that set out in that Form.

Preamble

C13–003 **2.1** This Protocol describes the behaviour the court will normally expect of the parties prior to the start of proceedings where a claimant claims damages valued at no more than £10,000 as a result of a personal injury sustained by that person in a road traffic accident.

Aims

C13–004 **3.1** The aim of this Protocol is to ensure that—
(1) the defendant pays damages and costs using the process set out in the Protocol without the need for the claimant to start proceedings;
(2) damages are paid within a reasonable time; and
(3) the claimant's legal representative receives the fixed costs at the end of each stage in this Protocol.

Scope

C13–005 **4.1** This Protocol applies where—
(1) a claim for damages arises from a road traffic accident occurring on or after 30th April 2010;
(2) the claim includes damages in respect of personal injury;

(3) the claimant values the claim at not more than £10,000 on a full liability basis including pecuniary losses but excluding interest ('the upper limit'); and
(4) if proceedings were started the small claims track would not be the normal track for that claim.

(Paragraphs 1.1(6) and 4.3 state the damages that are excluded for the purposes of valuing the claim under paragraph 4.1.)

(Rule 26.6 provides that the small claims track is not the normal track where the value of any claim for damages for personal injuries (defined as compensation for pain, suffering and loss of amenity) is more than £1,000.)

4.2 This Protocol ceases to apply to a claim where, at any stage, the claimant notifies the defendant that the claim has now been revalued at more than the upper limit.

4.3 A claim may include vehicle related damages but these are excluded for the purposes of valuing the claim under paragraph 4.1.

4.4 This Protocol does not apply to a claim—

(1) in respect of a breach of duty owed to a road user by a person who is not a road user;
(2) made to the MIB pursuant to the Untraced Drivers' Agreement 2003 or any subsequent or supplementary Untraced Drivers' Agreements;
(3) where the claimant or defendant is—
    (a) deceased; or
    (b) a protected party as defined in rule 21.1(2)(d);
(4) where the claimant is bankrupt; or
(5) where the defendant's vehicle is registered outside the United Kingdom.

4.5 The fixed costs in rule 45.29 apply in relation to a claimant only where a claimant has a legal representative.

SECTION II—GENERAL PROVISIONS

Communication between the parties

5.1 The address for electronic communication with the defendant **C13–006**
can be found at www.rtapiclaimsprocess.org.uk. The claimant will give an address for contact in the Claim Notification Form ('CNF'). Subject to paragraph 6.1(2) where the Protocol requires information to be sent to a party it must be sent electronically.

5.2 Where the claimant has sent the CNF electronically to the wrong defendant the claimant may, in this circumstance only, resubmit the CNF to the correct defendant. The period in paragraph 6.11 or 6.13 starts from the date the CNF was sent to the correct defendant.

Time periods

5.3 A reference to a fixed number of days is a reference to business days as defined in paragraph 1.1(8).

5.4 Where a party should respond within a fixed number of days, the period for response starts the first business day after the information was sent to that party.

5.5 All time periods, except those stated in—

(1) paragraph 6.11 (the insurer's response);

(2) paragraph 6.13 (MIB's response); and

(3) paragraph 7.30 (the further consideration period)

may be varied by agreement between the parties

5.6 Where this Protocol requires the defendant to pay an amount within a fixed number of days the claimant must receive the cheque or the transfer of the amount from the defendant before the end of the period specified in the relevant provision.

Limitation period

5.7 Where compliance with this Protocol is not possible before the expiry of the limitation period the claimant may start proceedings and apply to the court for an order to stay (i.e. suspend) the proceedings while the parties take steps to follow this Protocol. Where proceedings are started in a case to which this paragraph applies the claimant should use the procedure set out under Part 8 in accordance with Practice Direction 8B ("the Stage 3 Procedure").

5.8 Where the parties are then unable to reach a settlement at the end of Stage 2 of this Protocol the claimant must, in order to proceed to Stage 3, apply to lift the stay and request directions in the existing proceedings.

Claimant's reasonable belief of the value of the claim

5.9 Where the claimant reasonably believes that the claim is valued at between £1,000 and £10,000 but it subsequently becomes apparent that the value of the claim is less than £1,000, the claimant is entitled to the Stage 1 and (where relevant) the Stage 2 fixed costs.

Claimants without a legal representative

5.10 Where the claimant does not have a legal representative, on receipt of the CNF the defendant must explain—

(1) the period within which a response is required; and

(2) that the claimant may obtain independent legal advice, for example from a legal representative, a Citizens Advice Bureau, a local law centre or a trade union.

Discontinuing the Protocol process

5.11 Claims which no longer continue under this Protocol cannot subsequently re–enter the process.

SECTION III—THE STAGES OF THE PROCESS
Stage 1

Completion of the Claim Notification Form

C13–007 **6.1** The claimant must complete and send—

(1) the CNF to the defendant's insurer; and

(2) the 'Defendant Only CNF' to the defendant by first class post.

6.2 The 'Defendant Only CNF' must be sent at the same time or as soon as practicable after the CNF is sent.

6.3 All boxes in the CNF that are marked as mandatory must be completed before it is sent. The claimant must make a reasonable attempt to complete those boxes that are not marked as mandatory.

6.4 A claim for vehicle related damages will ordinarily be dealt with outside the provisions of this Protocol under industry agreements between relevant organizations and insurers. Where there is a claim for vehicle related damage the claimant must—

(1) state in the CNF that the claim is being dealt with by a third party; or

(2) (a) explain in the CNF that the legal representative is dealing with the recovery of these additional amounts; and

(b) attach any relevant invoices and receipts to the CNF or explain when they are likely to be sent to the defendant.

6.5 Where the claimant is a child, this must be noted in the relevant section of the CNF.

6.6 The statement of truth in the CNF must be signed by the claimant or the claimant's legal representative. Where the claimant is a child the statement of truth may be signed by the parent or guardian. On the electronically completed CNF the person may enter their name in the signature box to satisfy this requirement.

Rehabilitation

6.7 The claimant must set out details of rehabilitation in the CNF. The parties should at all stages consider the Rehabilitation Code which is set out in Annex D of the Pre–Action Protocol for Personal Injury Claims.

Failure to complete the Claim Notification Form

6.8 Where the defendant considers that inadequate mandatory information has been provided in the CNF, that shall be a valid reason for the defendant to decide that the claim should no longer continue under this Protocol.

6.9 Rule 45.36(2) sets out the sanctions available to the court where it considers that the claimant provided inadequate information in the CNF.

Response from insurer

6.10 The defendant must send to the claimant an electronic acknowledgment the next day after receipt of the CNF.

6.11 The defendant must complete the 'Insurer Response' section of the CNF ("the CNF response") and send it to the claimant within 15 days.

Application for a certificate of recoverable benefits

6.12 The defendant must, before the end of Stage 1, apply to the Compensation Recovery Unit (CRU) for a certificate of recoverable benefits.

Motor Insurers' Bureau

6.13 Where no insurer is identified and the claim falls to be dealt with by the MIB or its agents the CNF response must be completed and sent to the claimant within 30 days.

6.14 Where the MIB passes the claim to an insurer to act on its behalf, that insurer must notify the claimant of that fact. There is no extension to the time period in paragraph 6.13.

Contributory negligence, liability not admitted or failure to respond

6.15 The claim will no longer continue under this Protocol where the defendant, within the period in paragraph 6.11 or 6.13—

(1) makes an admission of liability but alleges contributory negligence (other than in relation to the claimant's admitted failure to wear a seat belt);

(2) does not complete and send the CNF response;

(3) does not admit liability; or

(4) notifies the claimant that the defendant considers that—

 (a) there is inadequate mandatory information in the CNF; or

 (b) if proceedings were issued, the small claims track would be the normal track for that claim.

6.16 Where the defendant does not admit liability under paragraph 6.15(3), the defendant must give brief reasons in the CNF response.

6.17 Where paragraph 6.15 applies the claim will proceed under the Pre-Action Protocol for Personal Injury Claims starting at paragraph 3.7 of that Protocol (which allows a maximum of three months for the defendant to investigate the claim) except that where paragraph 6.15(4)(a) applies the claim will proceed under paragraph 3.1 of that Protocol.

(Paragraph 2.10A of the Pre-Action Protocol on Personal Injury provides that the CNF can be used as the letter of claim except where the claim no longer continues under this Protocol because the CNF contained inadequate information.)

Stage 1 fixed costs

6.18 Except where the claimant is a child, the defendant must pay the Stage 1 fixed costs in rule 45.29 where—

(1) liability is admitted; or

(2) liability is admitted and contributory negligence is alleged only in relation to the claimant's admitted failure to wear a seat belt,

within 10 days after sending the CNF response to the claimant as provided in paragraph 6.11 or 6.13.

6.19 Where the defendant fails to pay the Stage 1 fixed costs within the period specified in paragraph 6.18 the claimant may give written notice that the claim will no longer continue under this Protocol. Unless the claimant's notice is sent to the defendant within 10 days after the expiry of the period in paragraph 6.18 the claim will continue under this Protocol.

Stage 2

The medical report

C13–008 **7.1** The claimant should obtain a medical report, if one has not already been obtained.

7.2 The claimant must check the factual accuracy of any medical report before it is sent to the defendant. There will be no further opportunity for the claimant to challenge the factual accuracy of a medical report after it has been sent to the defendant.

7.3 Where the claimant was not wearing a seat belt the medical report must contain sufficient information to enable the defendant to calculate the appropriate reduction of damages in accordance with principles set out in existing case law.

Initial medical reports

7.4 It is expected that most claimants will obtain a medical report from one expert. Where it is clear that one expert cannot deal with all elements of the injury the claimant may obtain a report from a second medical expert in a different discipline.

Further initial medical report on recommendation

7.5 Those two medical experts may each separately recommend that the claimant obtain a further initial medical report from a medical expert in a different discipline. Therefore the claimant may obtain a maximum of one initial medical report from four different disciplines, two of which are only on the recommendation of one or both of the first two medical experts.

Subsequent medical reports

7.6 On the recommendation of the medical expert who provided the initial medical report, a subsequent medical report may be obtained from that same medical expert. A subsequent medical report may be necessary—

(1) where the first medical report recommends that further time is required before a prognosis of the claimant's injuries can be determined; or

(2) where the claimant is receiving continuing treatment.

Stay of process

7.7 Where subsequent medical reports need to be obtained the parties should agree to stay the process in this Protocol for a suitable period. The claimant may then request an interim payment in accordance with paragraphs 7.8 to 7.11.

Request for an interim payment

7.8 Where the claimant requests an interim payment of £1,000, the defendant should make an interim payment to the claimant in accordance with paragraph 7.13.

7.9 The claimant must send to the defendant the Interim Settlement Pack and initial medical reports (containing the recommendation that a subsequent medical report is required) in order to request the interim payment.

7.10 The claimant must also send evidence of pecuniary losses and disbursements. This will assist the defendant in considering whether to make an offer to settle the claim.

7.11 Where an interim payment of more than £1,000 is requested the claimant must specify in the Interim Settlement Pack the amount requested, the heads of damage which are the subject of the request and the reasons for the request.

7.12 The interim payment of £1,000 is only in relation to general damages. Where more than £1,000 is requested by the claimant, the amount in excess of £1,000 is only in relation to pecuniary losses.

Interim payment of £1,000

7.13 Where paragraph 7.8 applies the defendant must pay £1,000 within 10 days of receiving the Interim Settlement Pack.

Interim payment of more than £1,000

7.14 Subject to paragraphs 7.17 and 7.18, where the claimant has requested an interim payment of more than £1,000 the defendant must pay—

(1) the full amount requested less any deductible amount which is payable to the CRU;

(2) the amount of £1,000; or

(3) some other amount of more than £1,000 but less than the amount requested by the claimant

within 15 days of receiving the Interim Settlement Pack.

7.15 Where a payment is made under paragraphs 7.14(2) or (3) the defendant must briefly explain in the Interim Settlement Pack why the full amount requested by the claimant is not agreed.

Vehicle related damages—interim payments

7.16 Claims for vehicle related damages will ordinarily be dealt with outside the provisions of this Protocol under industry agreements between relevant organisations and insurers. However, where the claimant has paid for the vehicle related damages, the sum may be included in a request for an interim payment under paragraph 7.11.

Application for a certificate of recoverable benefits

7.17 Paragraph 7.18 applies where the defendant agrees to make a payment in accordance with paragraph 7.14(1) or (3) but does not yet have a certificate of recoverable benefits or does not have one that will remain in force for at least 10 days from the date of receiving the Interim Settlement Pack.

7.18 The defendant should apply for a certificate of recoverable benefits as soon as possible, notify the claimant that it has done so and must make the interim payment under paragraph 7.14(1) or (3) no more than 30 days from the date of receiving the Interim Settlement Pack.

Request for an interim payment where the claimant is a child

7.19 The interim payment provisions in this Protocol do not apply where the claimant is a child. Where the claimant is a child and an interim payment is reasonably required proceedings must be started under Part 7 of the CPR and an application for an interim payment can be made within those proceedings.

(Rule 21.10 provides that no payment, which relates to a claim by a child, is valid without the approval of the court.)

7.20 Paragraph 7.19 does not prevent a defendant from making a payment direct to a treatment provider.

Interim payment—supplementary provisions

7.21 Where the defendant does not comply with paragraphs 7.13 or 7.14 the claimant may start proceedings under Part 7 of the CPR and apply to the court for an interim payment in those proceedings.

7.22 Where the defendant does comply with paragraph 7.14(2) or (3) but the claimant is not content with the amount paid, the claimant may still start proceedings. However, the court will order the defendant to pay no more than the Stage 2 fixed costs where the court awards an interim payment of no more than the amount offered by the defendant or the court makes no award.

7.23 Where paragraph 7.21 or 7.22 applies the claimant must give notice to the defendant that the claim will no longer continue under this Protocol. Unless the claimant's notice is sent to the defendant within 10 days after the expiry of the period in paragraphs 7.13, 7.14 or 7.18 as appropriate, the claim will continue under this Protocol.

Medical reports obtained without recommendation

7.24 Where a further initial medical report or a subsequent medical report is obtained without recommendation from a medical expert—

(1) the defendant at the end of Stage 2 may refuse to pay; or

(2) the court at Stage 3 may refuse to allow,

the costs of this medical report.

7.25 Brief details should be provided in the Stage 2 Settlement Pack Form—

(a) by the claimant explaining why they obtained a further initial report or a subsequent medical report without recommendation; and

(b) if relevant, by the defendant explaining why they will not pay for the report.

Submitting the Stage 2 Settlement Pack to defendant

7.26 The Stage 2 Settlement Pack which must comprise—

(1) the Stage 2 Settlement Pack Form;

(2) a medical report or reports;

(3) evidence of pecuniary losses; and

(4) evidence of disbursements (for example the cost of any medical report),

should be sent to the defendant within 15 days of the claimant approving the final medical report and agreeing to rely on the prognosis in that report.

7.27 Where the defendant alleges contributory negligence because of the claimant's failure to wear a seat belt, the Stage 2 Settlement Pack Form must also suggest a percentage reduction (which may be 0 per cent) in the amount of damages.

Consideration of claim

7.28 There is a 35 day period for consideration of the Stage 2

Settlement Pack by the defendant ("the total consideration period"). This comprises a period of up to 15 days for the defendant to consider the Stage 2 Settlement Pack ("the initial consideration period") and make an offer. The remainder of the total consideration period ("the negotiation period") is for any further negotiation between the parties.

7.29 The total consideration period can be extended by the parties agreeing to extend either the initial consideration period or the negotiation period or both.

7.30 Where a party makes an offer 5 days or less before the end of the total consideration period (including any extension to this period under paragraph 7.29), there will be a further period of 5 days after the end of the total consideration period for the relevant party to consider that offer. During this period ("the further consideration period") no further offers can be made by either party.

Defendant accepts offer of makes counter–offer

7.31 Within the initial consideration period (or any extension agreed under paragraph 7.29) the defendant must either accept the offer made by the claimant on the Stage 2 Settlement Pack Form or make a counter–offer using that form.

7.32 The claim will no longer continue under this Protocol where the defendant gives notice to the claimant within the initial consideration period (or any extension agreed under paragraph 7.29) that the defendant—

(a) considers that, if proceedings were started, the small claims track would be the normal track for that claim; or

(b) withdraws the admission of causation.

7.33 Where the defendant does not respond within the initial consideration period (or any extension agreed under paragraph 7.29), the claim will no longer continue under this Protocol and the claimant may start proceedings under Part 7 of the CPR.

7.34 When making a counter–offer the defendant must propose an amount for each head of damage and may, in addition, make an offer that is higher than the total of the amounts proposed for all heads of damage. The defendant must also explain in the counter–offer why a particular head of damage has been reduced. The explanation will assist the claimant when negotiating a settlement and will allow both parties to focus on those areas of the claim that remain in dispute.

7.35 Where the defendant has obtained a certificate of recoverable benefits from the CRU the counter–offer must state the name and amount of any deductible amount.

7.36 On receipt of a counter–offer from the defendant the claimant has until the end of the total consideration period or the further consideration period to accept or decline the counter offer.

7.37 Any offer to settle made at any stage by either party will automatically include, and cannot exclude—

(1) the Stage 2 fixed costs in rule 45.29;

(2) an agreement in principle to pay disbursements;

(3) a success fee in accordance with rule 45.31(1).

7.38 Where there is a dispute about the amount or validity of any disbursement the parties may use the procedure set out in rule 44.12A.

(Rule 44.12A provides that where the parties to a dispute have a written agreement on all issues but have failed to agree the amount of the costs, they may start proceedings under that rule so that the court can determine the amount of those costs.)

Withdrawal of offer after the consideration period

7.39 Where a party withdraws an offer made in the Stage 2 Settlement Pack Form after the total consideration period or further consideration period, the claim will no longer continue under this Protocol and the claimant may start proceedings under Part 7 of the CPR.

Settlement

7.40 Except where the claimant is a child or paragraphs 7.41 and 7.42 apply, the defendant must pay—

(1) the agreed damages less any—
  (a) deductible amount which is payable to the CRU; and
  (b) previous interim payment;
(2) any unpaid Stage 1 fixed costs in rule 45.29;
(3) the Stage 2 fixed costs in rule 45.29;
(4) the disbursements allowed in accordance with rule 45.30(2)(a); and
(5) a success fee in accordance with rule 45.31 for Stage 1 and Stage 2 fixed costs,

within 10 days of the end of the relevant period in paragraphs 7.28 to 7.30 during which the parties agreed a settlement.

(Rule 21.10 provides that the approval of the court is required where, before proceedings are started, a claim is made by a child and a settlement is reached. The provisions in paragraph 6.1 of Practice Direction 8B set out what must be filed with the court when an application is made to approve a settlement.)

Application for certificate of recoverable benefits

7.41 Paragraph 7.42 applies where, at the date of the acceptance of an offer in the Stage 2 Settlement Pack, the defendant does not have a certificate of recoverable benefits that will remain in force for at least 10 days.

7.42 The defendant should apply for a fresh certificate of recoverable benefits as soon as possible, notify the claimant that it has done so and must pay the amounts set out in paragraph 7.40 within 30 days of the end of the relevant period in paragraphs 7.28 to 7.30.

Vehicle related damages—additional damages

7.43 Paragraph 7.44 applies where, at the end of the relevant period in paragraphs 7.28 to 7.30 the claim ("the original damages") has not settled and there remain vehicle related damages ("the additional damages") being dealt with by a third party separate from the claim. The original damages include all elements of the claim in the existing Stage 2 Settlement Pack.

7.44 Where paragraph 7.43 applies the claimant must, in relation to the additional damages—

(1) notify the defendant that this separate claim is being considered;
(2) obtain all relevant information from the third party; and
(3) make a separate offer by amending the Stage 2 Settlement Pack Form.

7.45 Within 15 days of the claimant sending the offer under paragraph 7.44(3), the defendant must either agree the offer made by the claimant or make a counter–offer.

7.46 The counter offer must explain why a particular head of damage has been reduced to assist the claimant when negotiating a settlement and to allow both parties to focus on those areas of the claim that remain in dispute.

Original damages and additional damages are agreed

7.47 Where the original damages and additional damages are agreed within the period in paragraph 7.45 the defendant must pay the claimant in accordance with paragraph 7.53.

Original damages are not agreed, additional damages are agreed

7.48 Paragraph 7.49 applies where—

(1) the original damages are not agreed; but
(2) the additional damages are agreed.

7.49 Where paragraph 7.48 applies—

(1) the defendant must pay the agreed amount of the additional damages within 10 days of agreeing those damages, and
(2) claimant must continue with the provisions in paragraphs 7.55 to 7.66 of this Protocol.

Original damages are agreed, additional damages are not agreed

7.50 Paragraph 7.51 applies where—

(1) the original damages are agreed; but
(2) the additional damages are not agreed.

7.51 Where paragraph 7.50 applies—

(1) the defendant must, in relation to the original damages, pay the claimant in accordance with paragraph 7.53; and
(2) the claimant may start proceedings under Part 7 of the CPR in relation to the additional damages.

Original damages and additional damages are not agreed

7.52 Paragraphs 7.55 to 7.66 apply where the original and additional damages are not agreed.

Settlement after claim for additional damages

7.53 Except where the claimant is a child or paragraph 7.54 applies, the defendant must pay—

(1) the agreed damages less any—
    (a) deductible amount which is payable to the CRU; and
    (b) previous interim payment;
(2) any unpaid Stage 1 fixed costs in rule 45.29;

(3) the Stage 2 fixed costs in rule 45.29;
(4) the relevant disbursements allowed in accordance with rule 45.30; and
(5) a success fee in accordance with rule 45.31 for Stage 1 and Stage 2 fixed costs,

within 10 days of agreeing to pay the damages.

(Rule 21.10 provides that the approval of the court is required where, before proceedings are started, a claim is made by a child and a settlement is reached. The provisions in paragraph 6.1 of Practice Direction 8B set out what must be filed with the court when an application is made to approve a settlement.)

Application for certificate of recoverable benefits

7.54 Where at the date on which damages are agreed the defendant does not have a certificate of recoverable benefits that remains in force for at least 10 days the defendant should apply for a fresh certificate as soon as possible, notify the claimant that it has done so and must pay the amounts set out in paragraph 7.53 within 30 days of the date on which damages are agreed.

Failure to reach agreement—general

7.55 Where the parties do not reach an agreement on—
(1) the original damages within the periods specified in paragraphs 7.28 to 7.30; or
(2) the original damages and, where relevant, the additional damages under paragraph 7.45,

the claimant must send to the defendant the Court Proceedings Pack (Part A and Part B) Form which must contain—
(a) the final offer and counter offer from the Stage 2 Settlement Pack Form;
(b) supporting comments from both parties on disputed heads of damages; and
(c) relevant, the offer, and if made, the counter–offer under paragraph 7.45.

7.56 The deductible amount should only be deducted from the personal injury damages.

7.57 Comments in the Court Proceedings Pack (Part A) Form must not raise anything that has not been raised in the Stage 2 Settlement Pack Form.

7.58 The defendant should then check that the Court Proceedings Pack (Part A and Part B) Form complies with paragraphs 7.55 to 7.57. If the defendant considers that the Court Proceedings Pack (Part A and Part B) Form does not comply it must be returned to the claimant within 5 days with an explanation as to why it does not comply.

7.59 Where the defendant intends to nominate a legal representative to accept service the name and address of the legal representative should be provided in the Court Proceedings Pack (Part A) Form.

7.60 Where the defendant fails to return the Court Proceedings Pack (Part A and Part B) Form within the period specified in paragraph 7.58, the claimant should assume that the defendant has no further comment to make.

Non-settlement payment by the defendant at the end of Stage 2

7.61 Except where the claimant is a child the defendant must pay to the claimant—

(1) the final offer of damages made by the defendant in the Court Proceedings Pack (Part A and Part B) Form less any—
   (a) deductible amount which is payable to the CRU; and
   (b) previous interim payment

(2) any unpaid Stage 1 fixed costs in rule 45.29;

(3) the Stage 2 fixed costs in rule 45.29; and

(4) the disbursements in rule 45.30(2) that have been agreed.

7.62 Where the amount of a disbursement is not agreed the defendant must pay such amount for the disbursement as the defendant considers reasonable.

7.63 Subject to paragraphs 7.64 and 7.65 the defendant must pay the amounts in paragraph 7.61 and 7.62 within 15 days of receiving the Court Proceedings Pack (Part A and Part B) Form from the claimant.

7.64 Paragraph 7.65 applies where the defendant is required to make the payments in paragraph 7.61 but does not have a certificate of recoverable benefits that remains in force for at least 10 days.

7.65 The defendant should apply for a fresh certificate of recoverable benefits as soon as possible, notify the claimant that it has done so and must pay the amounts set out in paragraph 7.61 within 30 days of receiving the Court Proceedings Pack (Part A and Part B) Form from the claimant.

7.66 Where the defendant does not comply with paragraphs 7.63 or 7.65 the claimant may give written notice that the claim will no longer continue under this Protocol and start proceedings under Part 7 of the CPR.

General provisions

7.67 Where the claimant gives notice to the defendant that the claim is unsuitable for this Protocol (for example, because there are complex issues of fact or law in relation to the vehicle related damages) then the claim will no longer continue under this Protocol. However, where the court considers that the claimant acted unreasonably in giving such notice it will award no more than the fixed costs in rule 45.29.

Stage 3

Stage 3 procedure

C13–009 **8.1** The Stage 3 procedure is set out in Practice Direction 8B.

VOLUME 2

CIVIL PROCEDURE RULES

SECTION 6

ADMINISTRATION OF FUNDS, PROPERTY AND AFFAIRS

6A COURT FUNDS

Payment of money into a District Registry or county court

In rule 19, add new paragraph (1A):

(1A) The following persons may pay money into the Mayor's and City of London Court in accordance with paragraph (2)— **6A–66**

(a) a litigant in person without a current account who is involved in a claim proceeding at the Royal Courts of Justice; and

(b) a person who is required by or under any enactment to give security for costs in respect of proceedings for an election petition.

In rule 19(2), add after "paragraph (1)":

or (1A)

Note

Add at end:

and SI 2010/172

PART VII

PAYMENT, TRANSFER AND DELIVERY OF FUNDS OUT OF COURT

Payments out of money by post and identification of payees

In rule 40(9)(i), delete "the Court Funds Office or". **6A–93**

Note

At the end of the first paragraph add:

and SI 2010/172 **6A–94**

Transfer of funds from a special account to a basic account

Add new paragraphs 6A–105.2 and 6A–105.2.1:

6A–105.2 **45A.** When the Accountant General is notified, or becomes aware, that a person on whose behalf money is held in a special account ceases to be a person under a disability, the Accountant General shall transfer the balance of the special account to a basic account from the date the disability ceased.

Note

6A–105.2.1 Inserted by SI 2010/172.

PART X

UNCLAIMED FUNDS IN COURT

Unclaimed funds

Delete rules 57(2) and (3) and substitute:

6A–121 (2) Subject to paragraph (3), a fund shall be treated as unclaimed if—

(i) it stands to the credit of an account which has not been dealt with for a period of ten years otherwise than by the continuous investment or placing on deposit of accrued interest, the compulsory conversion, redemption or acquisition of securities or the placing on deposit of any money arising therefrom; or

(ii) the Accountant General is, at any time, satisfied that although all reasonable steps have been taken to trace the person entitled to it and to pay it to him, that person cannot be traced.

(3) Where a fund was lodged in court for the benefit of a child and—

(a) the child's date of birth is known, the rules mentioned in paragraphs 2(i) and (ii) shall not apply until the child's 18th birthday;

(b) the child's date of birth is not known, the rules mentioned in paragraphs 2(i) and (ii) shall apply from the date on which the fund is lodged in court.

Note

Add at end:

6A–121.1 and SI 2010/172

Lists of unclaimed funds

6A–122 *In rule 58(1) delete ", which may be inspected at the Court Funds Office during normal office hours".*

Note

At the end of the first paragraph, add:

6A–123 and SI 2010/172

Delete rule 59 and substitute:

6A–124 **59.** [...]

Note

Add at end:
and deleted by SI 2010/172 6A–124.1

Disposal of unclaimed securities in court

Delete rule 60 and substitute:

60.—(1)Where any securities (including common investment fund units) or effects are carried over under rule 57, the Accountant General may sell the securities or effects and pay the proceeds into the account of unclaimed balances. 6A–125

(2) The Accountant General shall write off any securities or effects carried over under rule 57 which have no value.

(3) Where any sum carried over under rule 57 stands to an interest bearing account, the Accountant General shall withdraw the sum and place it to the account of unclaimed balances.

Note

Add new paragraph 6A–125.1:
Amended by SI 2010/172. 6A–125.1

INDEX

LEGAL TAXONOMY

FROM SWEET & MAXWELL

This index has been prepared using Sweet and Maxwell's Legal Taxonomy. Main index entries conform to keywords provided by the Legal Taxonomy except where references to specific documents or non-standard terms (denoted by quotation marks) have been included. These keywords provide a means of identifying similar concepts in other Sweet & Maxwell publications and online services to which keywords from the Legal Taxonomy have been applied. Readers may find some minor differences between terms used in the text and those which appear in the index. Suggestions to *sweetandmaxwell.taxonomy@thomson.com.*

(All references are to paragraph number and all references to material in Volume 2 are enclosed in square parentheses)